Dear Sis, I Love You ...

An Anthology on Black Sisterhood

Dear Sis, I Love You ...

An Anthology on Black Sisterhood

CURATED BY

AMBER BOOTH MCCOY

KATINA BOOTH WHITE

Copyright © 2023 by Amber Booth McCoy and Katina Booth White.

All rights reserved. This book or any portion thereof may not be reproduced or used in any manner whatsoever without the express written permission of the publisher and authors except for the use of brief quotations in a book review.

Printed in the United States of America

First Printing, 2023

Library of Congress Control Number: 2022908814
ISBN (Hardback): 978-1-951883-90-4
ISBN (Paperback): 978-1-951883-91-1
ISBN (eBook): 978-1-951883-92-8

The Butterfly Typeface Publishing
PO Box 56193
Little Rock AR 72215

www.thebutterflytypeface.com

Dedicated to the …

Mothers Of Sistas
Sisters Of Sistas
Trans Sistas
Tired Sistas
Got It Together Sistas
Hurt Sistas
Joyous Sistas
Streetwalking Sistas
Afro Wearing Sistas
Growin-Edges-Back Sistas
Edges-Wont-Grow-Back Sistas
Loc Wearing Sistas
Permed, Sew In, Wig Wearing Sistas
Deeply Melanated Sistas
Corporate Sistas
Single Mother Sistas
Newly Married Struggling Sistas
Holding Space For My Sisters Sistas
We In This Together Sistas
Slow To Trust Sistas
We Soo Black Sistas
I Love Being Black Sistas

Sis, We Love You!

Black Sisterhood

To my Queen Mothers, Aunties, Sista-friends,
and all the Black Girl Magic flowing in spaces between:
In the immortal words of the beloved flawed character, Miss Shug Avery,
from the prolific story, *The Color Purple*:
"Sister, you've been on my mind.
Sister, we're two of a kind.
Oh sister, have I got news for you,
I'm something, I hope you think that you're something too…"

-Amber Booth McCoy

Table of Contents

Cortney Booth Akers..15
    Black Girl Magic Recipe..16

Foreword...17
    About Cortney Booth Akers (February 1990)..................................18

Veronica White..19
    Black Girl Magic Recipe..20

Foreword...21
    About Veronica White..22

Acknowledgments..23

Note From the Publisher...25

Introduction...27

Abdul-Bey, Clarice..29
    Black Girl Magic Recipe..30
    Dark As the Light..31
    About Clarice Abdul-Bey...33

Bailey Williams, Pamela "Bam"..35
    Black Girl Magic Recipe..36
    Dear Sis, I Got You...37
    About Pamela "Bam" Williams Bailey...41

Booth-McCoy, Amber..43
    Black Girl Magic Recipe..44
    Dear Sis, I Love You …..45
    About Amber Booth-McCoy...47

Booth White, Katina..49
   Black Girl Magic Recipe...50
   Black Sisterhood...51
   About Katina Booth White 54

Brooks, Akissi...55
   Black Girl Magic Recipe...56
   Godbition...57
   About Akissi Brooks..61

Davis, Alexis..63
   Black Girl Magic Recipe...64
   Hello Reflections...65
   About Alexis Davis...68

Davis, Coffy...69
   Black Girl Magic Recipe...70
   Ghetto Queen..71
   About Coffy Davis..74

Donnell, Rev. Dr. Denise...75
   Black Girl Magic Recipe...76
   What I Know..77
   About Reverend Denise Donnell..81

Essmorra..83
   Black Girl Magic Recipe...84
   Dear Black Woman Has Anyone Ever Told You?..........................85
   About Essmorra..87

Jackson, Sierra..89
   Black Girl Magic Recipe...90
   Sisterhood Ain't Easy, But It's Worth It...91
   About Sierra Jackson...93

Moka, Teresa, R...95
   Black Girl Magic Recipe...96
   A Designer's Original...97
   About Teresa R. Moka...98

Nazare, Vernice 99
    Black Girl Magic Recipe 100
    Friendship - The Long version 101
    About Vernice Nazare 106

Neal, Andrea L. 107
    Black Girl Magic Recipe 108
    A Few Things I've Learned 109
    About Andrea L. Neal 112

Okeke, Ngozika 113
    Black Girl Magic 114
    All That We Are 115
    About Ngozika Okeke 118

Olamide', Jionni 119
    Black Girl Magic Recipe 120
    To Infinity and Beyond 121
    About Jionni Olamide' 123

Pendelton, Jacqueline 125
    Black Girl Magic Recipe 126
    Enjoy the Small Things 127
    About Jacqueline Pendleton 129

Pettway LAC, Isis J. 131
    Black Girl Magic Recipe 132
    When Time Marches on and the New Arguments That Come Along with It 133
    About Isis J. Pettaway 135

Richardson, Casey Ariel 137
    Black Girl Magic Recipe 138
    All the Things I Couldn't Say 139
    About Casey A. Richardson 142

Sims, Nefatari 143
    Black Girl Magic Recipe 144
    Sisterhood 145
    About Nefertari Sims 149

Steward, April 151
   Black Girl Magic Recipe 152
   Dear Sis, I Love and See You 153
   About April Steward 154

Swift, Kalesha S. 155
   Black Girl Magic Recipe 156
   A Letter to the Younger Me 157
   About Kalesha S. Swift 159

Swift, Lyric N. 161
   Black Girl Magic Recipe 162
   Black Girl Magic – Beauty and Power 163
   About Lyric N. Swift 164

Taylor, Kara 165
   Black Girl Magic Recipe 166
   Black. Woman. Sister. 167
   About Kara Taylor 169

Tims, Kassidi 171
   Black Girl Magic Recipe 172
   Dear Kennedi 173
   About Kassadi Tims 174

Trichel, Kenzi 175
   Black Girl Magic Recipe 176
   Being A Woman 177
   About Kenzi Trichel 183

Wade, Vonetta 185
   Black Girl Magic Recipe 186
   Love, Support, and Forgiveness 187
   About Vonetta Wade 190

White, Jai 191
   Black Girl Magic Recipe 192
   Sisters and Loving 193
   About Jai White 194

Williams, Iris M. 195
    Black Girl Magic Recipe 196
    Giving 197
    About Iris M. Williams 200

Williams, Kendra 201
    Black Girl Magic Recipe 202
    My Iridium Sister 203
    About Kendra Williams 207

Wilson, Rayme 209
    Black Magic Recipe 210
    Beautiful You Are 211
    About Rayme C. Wilson 212

Wilson, Tudi 213
    Black Girl Magic Recipe 214
    What I Wish My Mom Had Told Me 215
    About Tudi Wilson 219

Writes, Drekkia 221
    Black Girl Magic Recipe 222
    When Is It Valid? 223
    About Drekkia Writes 226

Questions for Your Journey 227

Cortney Booth Akers

Black Girl Magic Recipe

Something Sweet: A puppy's kiss

Something Spicy: Louisiana Hot Sauce (I love hot sauce!)

Ancestor(s): Mary Booth (paternal grandmother)

Song: You Send Me by Sam Cook

Spirit Animal/Thing: White Coat

Mystery Ingredient: Jeremiah 29:11

For I know the plans I have for you," declares the LORD, "plans to prosper you and not to harm you, plans to give you hope and a future.

Foreword

Dear Amber,

God really did me a huge favor making you my big sister. Our relationship is the reason I am able to have long lasting friendships with others. You have taught me the true meaning of sisterhood. Sisterhood is a connection between two women that bonds their hearts together forever through respect, love, trust, and vulnerability. Christina Yang from *Grey's Anatomy* said it best, "You're my person." You are my best friend. You are an inspiration to all who meet you, a positive force to be reckoned with, and the best sister a girl could have. I pray that God continues to guide you to even higher heights. With God, there is nothing you can't do. You are my shero.

Love,

Cortney Booth, your sister
February 1990

About Cortney Booth Akers (February 1990)

Cortney Booth is an Arkansas native and the youngest daughter of Donald and Veronica Booth. Being a fierce lover of people and science, Cortney decided, at a young age, that healthcare and advocacy would be her life's focus. She narrowed her focus to Obstetrics and Gynecology after experiencing the birth of her nephew, Jaiden Barrett. Cortney graduated, with honors, from the prestigious Sewanee University with a Bachelor of Arts in Biology with a Political Science minor. After completing the undergraduate program, Cortney completed a research internship at the historic Yale Child Study Center and co-authored two prominent publications in the field of psychology. She also holds a Master of Arts in Biomedical Sciences from Lincoln Memorial University and received her Doctor of Osteopathic Medicine from DeBusk College of Osteopathic University. She is now in her last year of residency in Ob/Gyn at Oklahoma State University. Whether traveling abroad to perform routine health screenings to underserved populations, traversing Washington D.C. for DO Day on the Hill, or pounding the steps of Oklahoma State Capitol for ACOG Advocacy Day, Cortney continues to find the intersection of medicine and political advocacy.

In between being a stellar physician and fierce advocate for women, she is wedding planning. This fall, she will marry Kevin Akers in a ceremony and celebration of love, family, and forever.

VERONICA WHITE

Black Girl Magic Recipe

Something Sweet: Milk Chocolate

Something Spicy: Cajun Seasoning

Ancestor(s): A little bit of Martin & a whole lot of Malcolm

Song: ALL by Terrell feat. George Lovett & Saeed

Spirit Animal: Elephant

Mystery Ingredient: Confidence sprinkled with a few extra pounds

Foreword

My sister was my first best friend and come to think about it, she's actually my first cheerleader and encourager, the first person I had an agreement with, the first person to tell on me **insert side eye**. But unbeknownst to her, she was also my first role model and teacher. As the youngest, I looked up to my sister (I still do) and wanted to be just like her. She has taught me a lot by watching her up close and personal with a front row seat. As we grew into adulthood, we chose different paths, and Lord knows there are some things I wish I could go back and follow in my sister's footsteps. She's the family genius, and she birthed into this world the Gem of all Geniuses, my niece! She is the embodiment of BLACK GIRL MAGIC to the 10th power. She may have written the handbook on it **Insert eye wink**. She will always have my back, and I will always have her back. You better believe I'm going to have her front too. Most times, she doesn't think I pay attention to her, listen to her, or notice her accomplishments because I don't say anything. But if I could tell my sister anything in this world it would be: I SEE YOU, I HEAR YOU, I WATCH YOU, and I ADMIRE THE INCREDIBLE BLACK WOMAN THAT YOU ARE, and most of all, I LOVE YOU. I would not even be half the person I am today if I didn't have her as my big sister.

Know that I love you for LIFE!

Veronica "Ron" White, Your Little Sister
November 1981

About Veronica White

Veronica White (Gulley) was born and raised in Southwest Little Rock but is currently a native of Sherwood AR. She is a mother of one son who is her world. She loves all things makeup and plus size fashion (minus the heels because she can't walk in them…). She also enjoys playing softball and volleyball even through her knees checked out of the game a long time ago. Next up for Veronica is a digital project she is working on called "V's Diary," so be on the lookout.

Acknowledgments

to the DOPE Black Women who helped bring our vision to life

to our PATIENT ass publisher and team

to our AMAZING family

to the women who taught us to take up SPACE and held space for us

to Black SISTERHOOD

to GOD Herself

BLACK GIRL MAGIC

Note From the Publisher

Black Girl Magic, The Recipe

*W*hat *does Black Girl Magic mean to you?*

In my opinion, Black Girl Magic is a hip way of expressing that you are operating in your purpose. I believe it was the late Myles Munroe who said (loosely paraphrased), "… most successful creations are those that solve a problem."

When God said it was not good for man to be alone, He created woman. What an excellent way to solve a problem!

And I don't believe for one minute that our sole purpose is for the service of our mate. The Bible frequently uses the word man to reference mankind or in essence, the human race. Thus, we were all created to be of service to one another.

Determining how you are to serve is generally the issue.

Like most manufactured things, when used according to the manufacturer's specifications and recommendations, the level of operation is optimal.

When we are living in our purpose – that's when we experience **Black Girl Magic**!

Iris M. Williams

Butterfly Typeface Publishing,
Little Rock, Arkansas

Introduction

This collection of writings tells a beautifully-Black, wonderfully-flawed, eternally-redeeming, amazingly-affirming, purposefully authentic, and painstakingly-transparent story of Black sisterhood.

Each contributing sister curated a personally rich narrative, using her entire, multi-dimensional self as a literal or figurative tapestry for her lived experiences.

Dive into the stories of pain, passion, and promise that use sisterhood as the stage, melanin as the scenery and backdrop, and Black Girl Magic as the microphone.

Amber Booth McCoy

ABDUL-BEY, CLARICE

Black Girl Magic Recipe

Something Sweet: Yellow Flesh Watermelon (with SEED)

Something Spicy: Fresh Ginger Root Tea

Ancestor: Willie May Jackson (Maternal Grandmother)

Song: Laura Mvula Green Garden

Spirit Animal: Blue Morpho Butterfly

Mystery Ingredient(s): Moccasins & Comedy

Dark As the Light

Dear Sis,

This year has been like looking through a magnifying glass at every social, emotional, political, and spiritual aspect of my life. It has been both challenging and fulfilling. So much loss, yet we continue to thrive. We have no choice. For me, my family, loved ones, and "tribe" keep me centered. I am grateful for your love and support!

I have also made it my mission, as a wellness practitioner, to show up for my Black Indigenous People of Color (BIPOC) community in all the ways I know how. Some of the ways are through breath, voice, sound, and energy.

Melanin Mantras and Meditations is about setting focus and intention on who we are and how we present ourselves to ourselves. In other words, I am talking to myself about who I was created to be. I am encouraging myself. I am reminding myself that my life on this planet has value and purpose contrary to what I see and hear and have experienced.

I invite you to join me. We all have our self-doubting moments. Plugging into sacred words—tones—and vibrations can and will aid in our individual and collective wellness.

I am happy to share with you a link Meditations.mp4 to the audio/visual of one of the mantras and meditations written with you in mind.

I love you …

Clarice Abdul-Bey
November 1974

Dark as the Light

Clarice Abdul-Bey

You are dark as the light, beautiful and bright

Skin deep, blue-black, penny—red, golden honey, and tan—tight

How—I—love the way the sun sets a glow upon you

Look—at—YOU—(giggle) You (breath)—You are amassing, a song

One that is heard from tops of mountains and echoes through sunflower filled valley's

The wind whispers YOUR brilliance—and I agree

Hon—EY you are the spark, the flame…. the—ART

The spectrum of colors that reflects the light…Dark AS night…Dark as the light

About Clarice Abdul-Bey

Clarice Abdul-Bey is Afro-Indigenous and a native of Little Rock, Arkansas. She is the Co-Director of the Washitaw Foothills Youth Media Arts & Literacy Collective, and Co-Convener of the Arkansas Peace and Justice Memorial Movement (APJMM.org). As a lifelong youth mentor and youth advocate, Clarice is ardent about facilitating students in the areas of social emotional learning, using solutions-based journalism, interviewing skills, and what she likes to call active-empathetic listening techniques. In 2021, she was a U.S. cohort in the Building a Diverse and Inclusive Culture of Remembrance (DAICOR) Virtual Exchange Fellowship, a program created by Cultural Vistas in partnership with the Heinrich Böll Foundation. She is a proud AmeriCorps Alum in service (direct and VISTA) in the areas of food insecurity/justice and capacity building. As a Racial Justice Facilitator, Mental Health First Aider, and Mindfulness Relationships Practitioner, Licensed Massage Therapist, "Energy Liberator," and Trauma Informed Reiki Practitioner, Clarice is passionate about wellness integration in workspaces, advocacy, and social justice issues.

Bailey Williams, Pamela "Bam"

Black Girl Magic Recipe

Something Sweet: Mama's Black Walnut Banana Cake

Something Spicy: Louisiana Hot Sauce on Fish Fried Hard

Ancestor(s): My Grandma Arlene (*for her wisdom*)

Song: Don't You Worry 'Bout a Thing by Stevie Wonder

Spirit Animal: Phoenix (*bird of the sun reborn in the fire*)

Mystery Ingredient: Love (*it makes everything sweeter*)

Dear Sis, I Got You

Dear Sis,

Where you at now?

What are you doing now?

Girl, you can't sit down anywhere!

You better stop running from your calling!

Why do you think you need to go somewhere all the time?

 These are the questions and statements etched in the vinyl of my mind. A perpetual recording of interviews and *Law & Order*-style interrogations from friends and loved ones on holidays or catching up after a long overdue visit or phone call. Often presented as interest…sometimes perceived attempted sarcasm, however, intended…to those who know me best, I'm considered a "runner" of sorts.

 I didn't grow up with siblings. I had cousins who were like siblings. We lived close by…most my age were boys. So, I babysat my younger female cousins…often it was a group effort as the guys were their older brothers or cousins as well.

 I wouldn't say sisterhood came "natural" to me because, at a young age, I was outside climbing trees and hiking in the woods behind grandma's house with the fellas. My earliest female friend was a classmate of mine, whom I coincidentally slapped because she teased me about getting a higher grade on her spelling test. Her mom was subbing that day…in our classroom. Somehow, they both forgave me, and we had a friendship that lasted for years after…even playdates.

 So…yeah…I wasn't a girl's girl. Think Troy…Crooklyn Troy.

 Sass-mouthed and grown with my peers…surrounded by brothers…quiet and brooding around adults…protector of the younger ones…I can mess with them ALL DAY! But you CAN'T! Still.

 Daddy was a pastor…Mama was a supervisor of a store…and a first lady…

 Let the "preacher's daughter" jokes begin…Go ahead…I'll give you a minute…

Now.

Although I ran and played often as a child, I spent most of my middle school and high school years in fine arts electives and extracurricular activities. I don't have an athletic bone in my body, but my mind is an Olympic hopeful. It's like an infinite ring of ideas, observations, epiphanies, chatter, and bullshit. Cause let's face it…what's life without mindless humor and entertainment? It's taken over 40 years to accept myself and my ways as "normal." Without my sisterhood journey, I don't think I would have ever learned to love what others saw as my running, my faith, my tenacity, my fortitude, my femininity.

Cliques

Back in the 90s, if you were usually seen together, you were labeled a "clique." A clique was a group somewhat like a gang depending on where they hailed from…you just might get your tail whipped if you stepped wrong or became part of another community of families by association. I was never a part of that kind. I didn't really consider myself a part of any kind, but based on technicalities…even I know that's a lie. It's just that it offends my hyper-individualistic ideas about myself.

Very uncomfortable…I like thinking of myself autonomously floating from place to place loving all the people like a hippie minus the commune…because I still need my space.

My college years proved no different than my younger ones…I mostly hung with guys until I met a few girls in the dorm with whom I clicked. Although miles apart…we are still friends until this day.

But I never truly began to understand sibling dynamics until I joined Greek life. Before you jump to any conclusions, this is no ode to the Divine 9 or promotion of Black Greek life. On the contrary, it's where I began to learn that family doesn't always agree, that family has hypocrites, and that family has uncomfortable conversations, but they still love one another and show up for one another at the end of the day.

Online…the process of membership intake…we literally drove one another insane. With adult women ranging from ages 20-30+, there were a range of emotions and reactions daily. I often spent nights thinking…Lord, what have I done? Growing up around a lot of guys, I didn't have certain issues. I was the emotional one…if at all. Everything was resolved quickly, and males just moved on. No grudges…no shade…at least back then they just kept being bros to you. Boundaries were clear, and you never had to guess if they wanted anything, at least not my relatives.

Things were the opposite with women. There were more emotional triggers and landmines. A lot of times I sat in the group quietly until called upon. I like doing that a lot… even now. Kind of like that cat from the recipe, I like to move quietly throughout parties sitting in various spots observing behaviors and enjoying brief conversations.

I learned a lot watching my now sorors…I learned how women tick. Something I had never even thought about myself as a girl growing up, I just did stuff…never thinking gender specifically. But through an intense intake process, I learned quickly.

We were all so different yet the same in many ways. We had been raised in every style of family imaginable. There were 14 of us. Some by two parents, some by one, some by grandparents, and some by various family members in communal settings. Nevertheless, by timing and circumstance, we were now "sisters" of sorts.

As the years have gone by, those bonds have strengthened, broken, mended, healed, and settled in ways that showed me how to resolve conflict and how to let some things be. As one of my sisters says a lot, "It is what it is…" But one thing I can say for sure is that it's read. Always…even on days, you don't want it to be.

Getting Grown

So, there I sat with three of the line sisters in the courthouse waiting to file for divorce. We shared small talk and talked shit about the people in the office…not that they were so bad…but I needed to get my laugh on while what I knew as my world was ending. I sat there jobless, man less, and three children richer. All I had to my name was a Cadillac in need of multiple repairs. If you had told any of us 14 years earlier we'd be doing any of things we were doing in life, maybe one of us would have said, "Yeah, sure I knew." But there we were… older, wiser, nearing the end of our partying years with a little left in the tank.

I was 36 with a degree and no job thinking WTF just happened? That's something I still think a lot of days…nowadays. But I wasn't sitting there alone. As a matter of fact, those heifers had virtually helped me Underground Railroad my way out of an increasingly tumultuous relationship. Over the years, we had developed a rhythm of our own. Our friends and families had meshed and gelled into a network of sisters and mothers and aunties that supported us all. Because they knew I had nothing but my car and those kids, they were there to help me file for divorce.

It's not that they were happy about the occasion, it's that they were their sister's keeper. They wanted me happy, the way they met me; they wanted me whole. It was going to take years, but this was the STARTING point.

No matter where I moved, they kept in contact and watched over me. Some even whisked me away to ease the transition. When I needed an apartment…we found that together. When I needed furniture…they donated. Their mothers and brothers and fathers all pitched in whether it was a job or groceries or a ride. I never lacked because a sister always had my back.

Not just my sorors… I went from having a family of men to being a part of a sister circle that was larger and stronger than any romantic love I had ever known.

If I sat and named each woman who helped me out in a jam, who sat up late nights when I couldn't sleep, who told me that they saw something in me that I didn't see in myself, I'd miss someone for certain because discovering sisterhood and all of its struggles and triumphs has been just that rewarding.

Without my sisters from church, I would not have known that my voice was bold or that when I speak people listen.

Without my sisters in music, art, and poetry, I wouldn't know what interdisciplinary meant or that I had a gift worth sharing artistically. My friend Ebony, hooked me up with a mentor in the art world. Other women made sure we ate, had clothes that fit, and snacks on game days.

As a young tomboy, I never saw this coming. Sisters have bound me to a place of self-sufficiency and growth beyond description. They manifested the divine feminine in me.

I love you ...

Pamela "Bam" Williams Bailey
November 1977

About Pamela "Bam" Williams Bailey

Pamela "Bam" Bailey is a visual artist, a painter, and a poet from the American Deep South (rural Arkansas, Ouachita County, Highway 24). She is her parents' only child and is a daughter of the Diaspora North and South.

Bam's art, like her culture, is created from discarded and forgotten pieces. It is the amalgamation of American and Diasporic cultures and music that represents the entirety of the Black Indigenous American experience. From the Atlantic Slave trade…to the Birth of Hip-Hop culture…her art is symbolic of the endurance, creativity, and transformative nature of Blacks in the U.S. and the spread of a culture that was pieced together from the remnants of oppression and traditions passed along from our ancestors…"we are the mixed medium of humanity."

A masterpiece of American Culture.

Booth-McCoy, Amber

Black Girl Magic Recipe

Something Spicy: Pepper in the Thanksgiving greens

Ancestor(s): Audre/Zora/FannieLou and my great grandma

Song: Bigger by Beyoncé

Spirit Animal: Puma

Mystery Ingredient(s): Glitter and cuss words

Dear Sis, I Love You …

Dear Sis,

I am rooting for you, cheering for you, yelling for you, crying with you, fighting with you, sharing with you, growing with you, and laughing with you. I'm here when you need me and here when you don't.

Black Sisterhood has been one of the most special gifts in my life from being a big sister, to adopting big sisters, from pouring into younger sisters, and even understanding the value of sisters.

I'm in no way saying sisterhood is all candy canes, rainbows, glitter, laughs and sleepovers. Engaging in true sisterhood means there is potential for real hurt or harm because it requires vulnerability, and vulnerability is a responsibility we must honor with trust.

The world has developed narratives of Black women that may be true, and we often internalize: "strong Black woman", "angry Black woman", "vindictive and Jezebel Black women."

The truth is because of our experiences, families, communities, churches, and workspaces where our wholesale maybe hasn't been welcomed, possibly assaulted, sometimes ignored, often devalued, or worse silenced; it can often cause us to harden. We internalize the ideal of strength and trade in ability or even the desire to be soft. I challenge you to see other Black women as fragile, something we handle with care because we value each other.

My truth: when I would encounter soft spaces, supposedly "safe spaces," I wouldn't let my guard down because I didn't want to have to experience any unnecessary or additional hurts. What I have found is that my willingness to open up and experience space designed for Black women, centering Black women, simply for joy, restoration, and healing has contributed to my growth and my healing in ways I never would've known.

For me, Black sisterhood is at its simplest an affirming thread of magical connectivity pumping life and laughter into conversations and situations with little hope and everlasting exhaustion. At its grandest, it's an unexpected parachute, catching everything from fallen tears to deferred dreams with the smell of cocoa butter and the strength of snatched edges and grandma's prayers.

Black Sisterhood for me is a never-ending series of check-ins that gather me when I'm shaken, check me when I'm wildin', hold me when I'm healing, cover me when I'm bare assed, and plant me when I'm growing. At my best, I strive to pour into it what it has so graciously given to me, and at my lowest, I seek it like warm light during cold damp nights of life.

I want us to engage in a radical sisterhood that seeks to hold space for each other while also allowing ourselves to be seen by each other in all of our beauty and humanity. In my world, sisterhood is a full contact sport, not for spectators.

Remember the old African proverb, "If you want to go fast, go alone. If you want to go far, go together." Let's heal, grow, laugh…together.

I love you …

Amber Booth-McCoy
June 1985

About Amber Booth-McCoy

Amber Booth-McCoy is a native of Little Rock, Arkansas. She received dual degrees in psychology and sociology from U of A, Little Rock. In addition to the several professional/academic certifications she's received, Amber is currently working towards a terminal degree in Organizational Leadership with emphasis in Social Justice at Adler University. In March 2022, in recognition of her social justice efforts and community activism, Adler University awarded her the John Lewis, Good Trouble Scholarship, full tuition for the duration of her program. Amber served as an internal diversity, equity, and inclusion consultant for the largest academic research center in the State of Arkansas and has a decade of experience in higher education and healthcare. In 2017, Amber expanded her efforts towards influencing culture change by founding The Diversity Booth, Inc (TDB). TDB is an innovative inclusion, equity, and social justice consulting firm. TDB is experienced in co-creating sustainable, measurable, and inclusive cultures. Their diverse client portfolio includes several prominent international and national organizations.

Whether due to her eye-opening, TEDx, "Cause of Death: Kind and Colorblind," delivered spring 2020 or her DEI-centered written works found in *Forbes Magazine* and other well-known publications, Amber is considered an inclusive thought-leader in her field. She enjoys traveling to deliver DEI-centered keynote addresses, motivational speeches, guest lectures, etc. in an effort to disrupt and dismantle systems of oppression. Of all her many roles and responsibilities, Amber maintains, Mama. is by far the most rewarding and with an indescribable pay. She works zealously with the desire to see a world where everyone's sons and daughters are treated equitably, and their "pursuit of happiness" will never be impeded by hate or discrimination.

Booth White, Katina

Black Girl Magic Recipe

Something Sweet: A baby's laugh

Something Spicy: Sweet heat

Ancestor(s): Luvenia Mooney

Song: Imagine Me by Kirk Franklin

Spirit Animal: Eagle

Mystery Ingredient: Peace within

Black Sisterhood

Hey, sis. You see you?

No, sis!

I see you.

Hey sis, you feel safe?

No, sis!

I have space, sis.

Hey sis, you loving you?

Not today.

I love you, sis.

Hey sis, you give yourself grace today?

No, sis. I ran out.

Well, sis, I have enough for both of us.

Hey, sis, is your cup full?

No, sis, it's empty

Well, let me fill it up.

Why sis?

Because our journey is intertwined. You become me, and I become you.

Dear Sis,

Sisterhood is medicine. It's a warm coat in a cold, cruel world.

Black sisterhood is a Black woman's soul food. It satiates the soul.

I've never known a world without Black sisterhood.

We came out the womb two months apart, two years apart, born on the same day, brought into a family, ate Braums together, cried together, danced together, broke bread together, were broke together, fought together, fought for each other, fought and made up with each other, grew apart from each other, reconnected with each other, and held space for each other.

Black sisterhood has held me down when I was floating in the air about to jump off a cliff. It showed up in locked depressed bedrooms, held secrets of hurt that almost destroyed me, loved me out of suicide, and spoke beautiful things to ugly and damaging thoughts.

All I know is Black sisterhood.

We are an army.

We ride and die.

Happiness and love or encouragement and accountability,

I don't know anything else but Black sisterhood.

Been true to this. We ain't new to this; it's a glue to this. It's a community in this.

They warriors when I ain't,

"That's my sister, Knock this rock off my shoulder if you bad."

Backup for unplanned events,

"Sis, you need a babysitter?"

Know when you are good enough,

"Girl fuck him!"

Loving you out of anger,

 "YES, AND?"

Make you rest when my soul can't rest,

"You gon' kill yourself, stop!"

It's bearing witness to births of babies and dreams,

joy and pain, success and failures, blues and rhythms, hills and valleys, love and hurts.

I love you …

Katina Booth White
October 1979

About Katina Booth White

Katina White is a proud native of Little Rock, AR. Her love and enthusiasm for STEM and youth inspired her to obtain a degree in Middle Childhood Education with an emphasis in math and science. Katina began her career in education as an Integrated Science, Project Lead the Way, and Robotics Instructor. In this role, she successfully led multiple teams to regional and nationals awards in both VEX and BEST robotics.

Katina was awarded the 2018 Sherwood Teacher of the Year and the 2020 Forest Heights STEM Academy Teacher of the Year. Additionally, she was invited to be a keynote speaker for the 2018 March for Science. Katina serves as Vice President for the National Technical Association-Arkansas Chapter and on the DEI Committee for the National Association for Geoscience Teachers. Moreover, she was selected as one of twenty-five educators across the nation as a 2021 Ford Unsung Hero Award Recipient.

In 2021, Katina merged her passion for equity/inclusion and STEM by accepting an offer and opportunity from UAMS Division of Diversity, Equity, and Inclusion. UAMS is the largest academic health center in the state of Arkansas. She is the Inaugural Curriculum Coordinator for the UAMS Pathways Academy. This innovative and intentional initiative is a strategic collaboration with the Arkansas Division of Workforce Services Temporary Assistance for Needy Families Program. In this role, Katina spearheads curriculum design crafted to pique the interest of youth to one day shift the status quo of today's health care workforce. She's created several award-winning, nationally recognized, culturally relevant STEM programs and opportunities for grades K-undergraduate. Using multiple pedagogies, she co-creates intentional curricula tailored to impact and enrich historically excluded youth (minority, rural, low socio-economic, etc.) in underserved areas.

Katina is the mother of a beautiful, bright, and creative young girl named Jai. She considers motherhood her favorite way to serve. She continually aims to provide an environment that affords her daughter the gift of positive self-efficacy, self-esteem, and passion to learn.

It's this grounding that fuels Katina's passion to impact her community and students for the better. She truly believes that everyone possesses a gift and a light that must be shared with the world for us all to reach our greatest heights as a society. Her goal is to make sure that all children be given the tools and provided the opportunity to let their lights shine and become unapologetic about who they were created to be "A Manifestation of Greatness!"

BROOKS, AKISSI

Black Girl Magic Recipe

Something Sweet: My personality

Something Spicy: My authenticity

Song: Just Fine by Mary J. Blige

Ancestor(s): Mary McCleod Bethune

Spirit Animal: Owl

Mystery Ingredient: Ambitious Girl MAGIC!

Godbition

Dear Sis,

My name is Akissi, and while I am most known for the work I do with women and girls around the world, I am personally familiar with insecurities, imposter syndrome, feeling unworthy, unqualified, unfulfilled, and more. I am also familiar with being loved on, supported, uplifted, and growing with others who shared of the same shortcomings and flaws that I did. These others that I refer to are beautiful Black sisters whom I am forever grateful to have in my life, sisters who are different yet also one in the same, sisters just like you!

I have always loved taking pictures, but there was nothing to smile about in the pictures being taken of me at the police station after my ex-boyfriend attacked me. I was only 19-years old, and while it was not the first time I had to be taken to the hospital to be treated for injuries caused by him, it was the first time I told the truth and pressed charges. While most of my peers were enjoying their college experience, I was struggling during mine trying to balance being a full-time student and working full-time as I was physically, emotionally, financially, and mentally abused. I was so wrapped up in trying to love, understand, pull up and change my boyfriend for the better that I was pulling myself down. Yet no matter what I endured, I was very good at tuning out the bad to focus on my goals. No matter what, I continued to stay persistent in pursuing them. After moving on campus my sophomore year, I was surrounded by goal-oriented peers like myself 90% of the time, which only left 10% to be with my boyfriend. This allowed me to realize my worth and how better I was without him. The following fall, I broke up with him for good, and that is what led to my last attack. Prior to this incident, only a few people knew of the abuse, and after hiding it for so long, I was ashamed, disappointed, and I felt broken. I had so many emotions that drained me, and the main word to describe how I felt is *"empty,"* which is defined in "Webster's Dictionary" as *"having no real purpose or value."* I did not want to go back to my college campus with bruises, scars, black eyes, and even worse a broken spirit. I did not have the strength to hide my struggle or fake my smile. I felt that everything I endured the past few years was written all over me for others to read.

Although I pressed charges against him, it did not stop my ex-boyfriend from trying to contact or taunt me, and I am grateful to my college sister-friends who loved on and helped me to continue moving forward! It was no longer easy for me to resort back into the cycle of letting him back in my life because I was now held accountable in a supportive way by those who loved me.

Four months after the attack, we went to court, and my ex-boyfriend was ordered to stay away from me. My abusive experiences with him knocked me down, but they did not knock me out. When I left the courthouse that day, I felt FREE! I had this feeling of passion in my heart that I could not explain. I did not understand anything about purpose at that time, but I had a strong desire to help girls and young ladies grow! While a great load was lifted from my life by ending that chapter, I developed a desire to be accepted by others. Three years later, I began seeking the likes and approval of others by competing in pageants with hopes of winning a crown to prove myself! One of the requirements for the pageant was a platform, and I decided to create a workshop for teen girls. Through my platform, I found that my love for helping girls meant more to me than competing in a pageant, and I chose to build a foundation for the benefit of girls instead of sponsors for myself to compete in pageants. Those initiatives led to the founding of Ambitious Girls, Inc., an international serving organization.

For over half of my life, I was overly ambitious, and my ability to tune out struggles to focus on success led to an addiction for accomplishments. I set an unrealistic level of perfection that I passed off as ambition. I unintentionally used my ambition as a mask to hide my insecurities, mistakes, and more, but no matter what I accomplished, achieved, or overcame, I still felt incomplete. After years of being the mentor, motivator and go to person for others, I was missing something in my own life, and I was burned out on trying to do things my way. While I have succeeded in serving thousands of women and girls, my journey does not exempt me from experiencing "*life happens*" struggles in my personal life, but no matter how hard things are, I continue to GROW through, up, on, and forward. At least up until what I like to refer to as "Bittersweet 2016," this season was bitter, as here I was with the weight of the world on my shoulders because life as I knew it was turned upside down, again. I often criticized myself for my circumstances and felt that I was no longer able to continue in my purpose. Who was I to continue mentoring anyone? This season was also sweet because this was the season I was blessed to encounter 5 amazing Black women, 3 who have grown to be my sisters and 2 who have been better than mentors to me. These are 5 women who I was able to be vulnerable, open, and honest with and best of all, learn from and grow with. Success is not in the number of people or time served. Success is learning what and how to gain from our struggles to pour strength into those we are called to serve.

Godbition is the ambition to live the life that God created us for, and it was also during my season of "Bittersweet 2016" that I learned to live a Godbitious Lifestyle. We are often told that it is possible to overcome struggles, but we get stuck not knowing how to deal with the doubt that is caused by the struggles we don't admit we have. I had a hard time knowing I was purposed to be a life changer but doubting myself because my struggles made me feel disqualified. No matter how great we are at what we do, we are not exempt from struggles, and we shouldn't want to be. To struggle means to *"proceed with great effort,"* and when we allow them, our struggles not only teach us how to overcome obstacles but to identify the ones we create ourselves.

Sisterhood has a major impact on the struggles that I have overcome. It was during one of the most challenging seasons of my life that God blessed me with sisters who helped change my life. Growing through my struggles with my sisters allowed me to **grow** on from past experiences that led to me wearing a mask; **grow** up from bad habits that made me doubt myself; and continue **growing** forward in my purpose of helping women and girls do the same.

Dealing with doubt requires accepting that while being a Black woman is rewarding, it does not mean we will always be confident. Learning to be confident in God, instead of confident in ourselves is key. As Black women, we all have our own uniqueness, and while growing through my doubt, I learned that mine is Ambitious Girl MAGIC! Each day, I choose to be *"Motivated And Growing In Confidence."* When I was struggling, it was because I was trying to be overly ambitious, but I learned to be ambitious in God's works as He created each of us in His image with a purpose to serve Him. 2 Peter 1:3 teaches us that, "God's divine power has given us everything we need for a godly life through our knowledge of him who called us by his own glory and goodness." In learning this, I was also able to deal with doubt by growing in living for God daily, which does not equal perfection. Most of our doubt is grown from mistakes that we hold against ourselves and dealing with it requires forgiving ourselves just as we are taught to do when offended by others. As I was stripped of my cover ups, dealt with my insecurities, flaws, and learned to forgive myself, it was not easy. It seems like the more I grew, the more mistakes I made, but I still desired to be true to who God created me to be. No matter how ugly my truth was I began to own it. I went from being ashamed about people seeing my scars to caring more about them healing than my hiding them.

I began learning to deal with doubt by letting go of the level of perfection I set for myself! Learning my identity in God gave me confidence in Him to remove my mask. Each day, I strive to grow in being who our Lord God created me to be. One of my favorite meditating scriptures is Psalm 51:10 "Create in me a clean heart, O God, and renew a steadfast spirit within me."

One of the best things that helps me continue to deal with doubt is making God's assignments my ambitions and His directions my desires while continuing to embrace my sisters, their flaws, shortcomings, and mistakes just as I embrace and work through my own. I encourage every woman and girl reading this to love on your sisters near and far and at the same time, allow them to love you back. There is a special love shared between Black women that is like none other. We need each other. We are the pieces of the puzzle that make up the whole picture.

I love you … (*but there is no one in this world who will love you more than you!*)

Akissi Brooks
birthdate

About Akissi Brooks

Akissi Brooks is the owner of Ambitious Girl Avenue, LLC, a firm that offers professional coaching and consulting services, personal office suites, and rental space for women. Akissi is also the founder of Ambitious Girls, Inc., a National Promising Practice Organization recognized by the Character Education Partnership in Washington, D.C. Akissi believes "All girls are ambitious, and every girl is an Ambitious Girl." In December 2019, Akissi launched the first international chapter of Ambitious Girls, Inc. in Ghana, West Africa. To date, thousands of girls in the United States, South Africa, and West Africa have been empowered by initiatives under the Ambitious Girl platform. Akissi is a lifetime learner who believes the more we know the more we can teach and help others to grow! She fulfills her passion of this belief as a college business professor, speaker, trainer, and life coach. Akissi's words of wisdom are "Sometimes we have to **grow** through things to make them RIGHT when they are WRONG, and EASY when they are HARD." While she is known by many as "Ambitious Akissi," before the Ambition, Akissi is simply a woman who values her family, appreciates her friends, enjoys traveling, writing, and strives daily to be obedient to God who is the center of it all!

Davis, Alexis

Black Girl Magic Recipe

Something Sweet: Peaches, Peach cobbler

Something Spicy: Stuffed jalapeños

Ancestor(s): Marcus Garvey and Eartha Kitt

Song: If This World Were Mine by Luther Vandross

Mystery Ingredient: Loud laughs & Bubble baths

Hello Reflections

ear Sis,

I open my eyes, and I finally choose to see you. I mean ALL of you, every part that makes you who you are. I see how your eyes done changed, hazy from all that loud. Loud noise keep you stuck in a haze. Love lost set your heart ablaze. But damn, you still get up and smile. How magical is that? I just want you to know that your smile don't have to hide your pain. I want to make space for you to feel again. I mean feel it ALL, especially the good stuff cause honey looking in your eyes I see your soul needs a resting. So be more mindful of all the blessings. I know lessons are coming too. Just remember that this is temporary, and you are your strongest you.

I open my eyes, and I finally choose to see you. I mean ALL of you. Dear beautiful, stop tearing yourself down to "get yourself together." You aren't broken. In fact, you are a beautifully woven quilt of experiences with blood sweat and tears sewn into the seams. I mean my dear mermaid you are the abundance of the ocean. Your eyes are the pearl of the sea. I know sometimes it seems rough. That I won't deny. It's not easy being you. I will give you all of that. And at the same time, I choose to acknowledge the divinity it takes for you to wake up every day and be.

Be, hmmm be, be free. Be you. Be love. Be truth. Be water. Be fruit. Be soft with yourself. Be kind. Be compassionate. Be wise. Be bold. Be brave. Be ok with not being ok. Be comforted in all your ways, trusting that you are guided and protected. Be all that you manifested to be.

Please just be.

Breathe and be. Love and be. See and be. Grow and be.

Breath.

I open my eyes, and I finally choose to see you. I mean I see the competitiveness. I also see this tendency to see what falls short and very seldomly noticing the bridges and highways that make up the distance for the shortage. I see how you are learning to celebrate yourself more. I am seeing how you are learning more about who you are in all essences of the form. I see you opening up more, even though it's scary. I see you doing more things that once were scary. I see you learning parts of yourself you never allowed yourself to explore. I see you enjoying love and being love and giving love. I see you hurting sometimes. I see you coping sometimes. I see you smoking sometimes. Puff. Puff. PASS. I see you passing on things that no longer serve you while still learning lessons in certain areas. Commitment. Discipline. Consistency.

Communication. Three Cs and a D baby, you working on it.

I open my eyes and finally choose to see you. I mean all of you. I see you learning to forgive yourself. I see you working to forgive others, learning to let shit go. Stop ruminating and open to new experiences. I see you floating above all the worldly materials and choosing peace. I see you releasing fear and moving more into joy and peace. I see you shedding the weight that has held you down. I see you. I … see … you. I see you, and that's liberating. If I see you, then you see me. I think I'm the highest part of you. I'm seeing you and calling you higher.

I opened my eyes and finally chose to see you, ALL of you. I see you answering the call even if the network isn't always clear. I see you figuring out your purpose more. I see you learning to go after your dreams. I see you knowing that you are capable of not only envisioning your dreams, but you're also capable of accomplishing them too, beyond your wildest imagination.

I opened my eyes and finally chose to see you. I see ALL of you. I know that for a moment there you took a snooze from life. That's ok. You're up now, and you rise naturally, no more snooze. I see you, Queen. I'm basking in the beauty of your soul, the trails of your tears, the fire in your fears. I'm taking in all of you and allowing you to take up space in the way you need to.

I see you, and I love you. I see you, and I forgive you. I see you, and I choose YOU, ALL OF YOU. I see you, and I smile. I see you, and I hug you. I see you, and I root for you. I see you, and I get you. I see you, and I release you from low vibrations. I see you, and I raise you higher. I see you, and I increase your knowledge of who you are. I see you, and I love you, sis. I really do. I see you, and I celebrate you. I celebrate all the loud and silent battles you've won. I see you, and I'm grateful you've let go of the suicide.

Suicide.

Suicide.

I open my eyes, and I see you. I see you choosing life every day. I see you struggling with that sometimes. I see you fighting off shit that nobody knows about. I see you crying your way through. I see you rising above those thoughts and trusting you more. I see you conquering your fears to live. I see you living. I see you winning over suicide. Remember, I SEE YOU.

It's ok to be seen.

Seen.

I open my eyes and I see you vulnerable, naked, unapologetic, all of you and all your moods. All of you and all the dips and curves of your body, I opened my eyes and chose to see you.

Again, know I see ALL of you. It's a beautiful rendition of Innervisions and Songversations.

Medicine for the soul, I see you. You're a balm and the bomb, love, light, and balance of the darkness. I see you. I see some things you had to go through. They happened for you.

I open my eyes. Take a deep breath and I realize

I am not just my mother's daughter. I am my mother.

I'm not just my grandmother's, granddaughter. I am my granny. I'm not just my sister's keeper; I am my sister.

I take another deep breath. I give myself a hug. I take a deeper look into the mirror and say, "Hello Reflections."

I love you ...

Alexis Davis
February 1991

About Alexis Davis

Dr. Alexis Davis is the founder of BBLVK Jewel which is a community organization that aims to highlight the jewels in the community serving people of African descent. Be sure to go check out BBLVK Jewel's podcast on all streaming platforms (Apple, Spotify, SoundCloud, etc.). Dr Alexis Davis provides professional and personal development training on Cultural Humility, working with clients of African descent, Hip Hop Healing workshops, as well as workshops on transgenerational trauma and healing among people of African descent.

In 2020, Dr. Davis made the decision to relocate to the continent to grow and learn Black/African psychology and the global healing and liberation of African people from the soil of our ancestors. She has held retreats, volunteered, and developed and hosted a 10-week women's program. Dr. Davis also provides these services virtually and is excited to have fellow fear-flexers come and retreat with her.

Davis, Coffy

Black Girl Magic Recipe

Something Sweet: My mom's lemon meringue pie with Jackson vanilla wafer crust

Something Spicy- Spicy cauliflower

Ancestor(s): Ntozake Shange (*the choreopoem goddess*)

Song: Extraordinary Being by Emeli Sande

Spirit Animal: Cat (*the almighty feline energy is strong in me*)

Mystery Ingredient: A Gumbo of creativity, passion, drive, and discipline

Ghetto Queen

ear Sis,

(Excerpt from Ghetto Politics poetry book)

I was famous for my smile.
My laugh was an acoustic sound that was caught in my throat
A tangle of down-home soul
And the ghettos of the west coast.
It came from my gut
Like Arkansas Gospel,
But I had an Oakland attitude that was abrupt and hostile
Young and wild.
I was *honeybabychild*
The one with the flip mouth
On the monkey bars hanging upside down
Counting cumulous clouds
Stretched out on a mattress
In the back of an old house in headphones
Opening subliminal love notes sent from Nina Simone
Cause her melancholy tone made it easy for me to sing along.
She knew what it was like to sit in the eye of the storm.
I read Langston Hughes poems,
And he hung a string of pearls around my neck
And called me his sweet brown Harlem girl
In a southern dialect.
When Ray and I met, he gave me his sight for one night

and sang me to sleep
On a sad and sweet serenade.
Teachers' eyebrows were raised when I came as Billie Holiday
For the Halloween parade in the 6th grade.
I was student, but I even knew then
That Huey Newton stood on the same streets that I played.
He wore a black beret,
And I wore Gucci braids, but we both had eyes that could articulate.
He was legacy, and I was destiny, and together we'd be great.
See, life is the perception that I create.
So, I'd lay awake with gunshots outside my window,
But I could hear the wind blow.
I could feel the sun kiss my forehead in midafternoon in the ghetto.
I counted dandelion dreams out of weeds
Where flowers ain't even supposed to grow.
Shoot, I picked a wild Irish rose
And watched the sunset in soprano.
I saw Kings lean in thrones of woodgrain and chrome
And watched Picasso and Michelangelo paint in graffiti
In beautiful bold strokes
Warriors walking alone thru winding roads
Hood heroes in Velour track suits
Boys who shot all their hope into basketball hoops.
I walked thru gravel pastures
And paused to hear the familiar laughter
From hide n go seek.
I felt the pulse of the street, and it was the beat
That made me switch in my Guess jeans
And black and red Jordans moved to a cadence beat.
My body rocked in synch with hopscotch
And Orange Crush pop,
And every brother remembers me.
I'm Ghetto Queen.
I jumped off the cliff and on the way down made wings.

I'm Ghetto Queen.

Mama, can't you see?

God shed His grace on me.

I was young, Black, and gifted.

I had a 6th sense.

I could hear the universe whispering.

I had the world listening.

Their intellect hid behind my genius.

So, they tried to capture my world as ghetto lore.

I watched as the things that I wore

Become things I can't even afford anymore.

See, I'm Ghetto Chic

An urban sophisticate.

I put an extra sway to my hips, peach body spray and French tips,

And suddenly, struggle becomes hip.

So, I'm forced to try to fit in with my own trends

Or start a new thing.

I watch as the stars line up behind me.

Took me years to realize that I was the light and others should find me,

I watch project princesses laugh and cry

And hand them their life back when I write.

I place ribbons over the sky in the hood.

I will not let us be misunderstood

Beautiful Black and Free

Lovely

And proud to be a Ghetto Queen.

I jumped off the cliff,

But on the way down, I made wings

Ghetto Queen.

Mama, can't you see?

God shed His grace on me.

I love you …

Coffy Davis, February 1976

About Coffy Davis

Coffy is the founder of The Underground Railroad Neighborhood Project (T.U.R.N. Project), an initiative that bridged art and literacy with at-risk communities. She first became known for her regional stage play, "FREEDOM," a play that merged verse and performance.

Coffy is also the visionary behind The March for Black Women & Girls (Arkansas Chapter, USA).

Coffy's book, MEdusa: Reflections of an Angry Black Girl, won awards with the Arkansas State Arts Council Award for Creative Non-Fiction and the Nan Snow Emerging New Writer's Award.

She also has written two books of poetry, Ghetto Politics and MEdusa: Reflections in Poetry.

Coffy is a yoga instructor and a fitness expert. She currently speaks at events that center around the empowerment of women and girls, fitness, self-care, and writing through trauma.

Donnell, Rev. Dr. Denise

Black Girl Magic Recipe

Something Sweet: A tender kiss on the forehead

Something Spicy: My personality

Ancestor(s): Audre Lorde

Song: Stand Up, by Cynthia Erivo

Spirit Animal: Butterfly

Mystery Ingredient: Intuition

choose joy

What I Know

ear Sis,

*You're not bold enough for me
Not strong enough in your shoes
To stand up to me*

        my wit
           my intelligence my candor

You're not confident enough of me

Not confident enough to believe yourself worthy

        *to believe yourself lovable to
        know yourself wanted*

*No way you value me
You don't know its power*

Your soul has yet to be kissed by its presence

Your spirit emblazoned by its speech

You're not available to me

*Your mind closed to possibilities
because you cannot imagine*

        cannot imagine you beyond your self
          *me beyond myself us
          beyond ourselves*

*You're unable to touch the sky
to straighten your arm*

*to reach until it hurts
to wiggle your fingers*

until they touch the fringes of newness
       of light
       of what can't be seen

only felt
only sensed
only
known

You can't have
me as companion

as friend
as lover

as confidante
as seer

You can't have me as
partner

tongue twister
mind bender

My knowledge is too high
understanding too vast
analysis too deep thinking
too complex
I have a choice to make

Walk away and Breathe
or

Stay and Collapse

Collapse into

arms stretched wide
a body freely given

a life made convenient
many roads well-traveled

I confess. I paused
contemplated, weighed
my options

My mind refused to decide

Donnell, Rev. Dr. Denise

It couldn't make the leap, so I closed it

Then, I exhaled

My body knew to breathe even when my mind didn't
That's when I knew

I walked
away Bold
Confident
Strong

Valued
Loved

Everything you are not

And can't seem to become

I should feel ashamed for being 49 years old before I was able to pen these words, but I don't. I don't because this world no longer dictates my life. It does not define me, cannot approve of me, cannot validate me, cannot deem me worthy, and cannot tell my story. My body belongs to me as yours belongs to you. The greatest gift we can give to ourselves is to remain open, honest, vulnerable, and transparent in our relationships with ourselves, with our bodies. Body, mind, spirit…that is the Holy Trinity we must hold sacred and honor every single day.

But let's say you don't.

I want you to know that is okay.
You are okay.

You are loved.

You deserve respect and to live a life of dignity anyway.
There is no "right" way to live.
Pave your own path.

There is no "wrong" way of living. Chart your own course.

Life is about choices. Some choices yield better outcomes than others. Make your choices. Learn from them. Live through them. Grow even more on the other side of them.

Enjoy every moment along the way.
Be unapologetic with your joy.

Be gracious with your love.

Be careful who you allow to love you. Not everyone is worthy of your love. Not everyone is worthy of your presence. Not everyone deserves your help. Not everyone can handle the beauty of your mind.

That is okay.
You are
okay.

You will always be okay. Just remember to breathe.

When life is hard, breathe. When feeling disrespected, breathe. When frustrated by the evil ways of the world, breathe. For it is in the inhale and the exhale that your mind regulates your body, stilling you enough so that you can make the more intelligent decisions. That makes the way you fight back strategic, intentional, and effective. Your breath makes it possible for you to stand strong and brave and bold at all times, in all places, in front of all people, especially your people, particularly your sisters.

Though you owe us nothing, we are with you. We are connected to you. You are connected to us. We are one. What happens to you happens to me. What happens to me happens to you. We carry each other not only on our backs, but in our cells. Your soul holds mine. My soul holds yours. We love each other. We are love for each other. Remember that. Let that love for you, that love for us guide you. Let it guide you into all truth. Let it lead you to freedom. Let it secure your liberation. And along the way, don't forget to laugh. Laugh loudly from the bowels of your belly. Laugh so loudly it interrupts conversations. Laugh so carelessly it causes jealous stares. Laugh so freely it inspires. If nothing else, let the mark you leave on the world be one of laughter and joy and love and light. That is enough. You are enough. You … are … enough.

I love you …

Reverend Denise Donnell
May 1972

About Reverend Denise Donnell

Denise Donnell navigates life inspired by a spirit of excellence that seeks to come alongside everybody on the journey toward collective liberation. As founder and Senior Strategist for jusTalk Consulting, Denise has dedicated this season of her life to traversing the truth. Uniquely poised by systems of domination, exclusion and oppression, Denise partners with individuals and collectives, profits and nonprofits, the sacred and the secular to foster intra and interpersonal dialogues that ultimately affect systemic change.

Essmorra

Black Girl Magic Recipe

Something Sweet: Pralines with extra nuts

"Life is a sweet gift, and I appreciate the bumps."

Something Spicy: A dash of red chili flakes to keep it a *lil* spicy

Ancestor(s): Permission to speak is given from ancestors known and unknown

Spirit Animal: Bull

Mystery Ingredient: Colorful language & Homemade Florida water

Dear Black Woman Has Anyone Ever Told You?

ear Sis,

Black woman,

I love you.

Black woman, I appreciate you

I thank Goddess for you

And give thanks to you

For all your love that's unconditional

And the love that came with understood conditions.

That's never been mentioned.

No one ever told you how much your heart would ever have to bear.

You just did that shit

Because you care.

Bent

Twisted

Folded

But never contained to fit one mold.

Even when you're told how to be,

Black woman, you inspire me.

You inspire the world.

The universe lives between your thighs

Orion's galaxy in your eyes foreseeing the next shift.

Crowds tower around you because you are the ultimate gift

to humanity

Balancing out recurring turmoil with

Love, patience, and forgiveness.

Black woman, you are resilient.

The next time you need a reminder look in the mirror.

Black woman, you are BRILLIANT!

I love you …

Essmora
May 1990

About Essmora

Essmora writes to help her let go of things. She writes to remember things. Writing helps her heal or laugh; sometimes writing simply helps to get a thought down that she thought was cool.

Writing allows her to voice what she struggles to say sometimes.

Writing allows her to make what she wants to happen and brings her truth to light.

Jackson, Sierra

Black Girl Magic Recipe

Something Sweet: Chocolate Turtles

Something Spicy: Jalapeños

Ancestor(s): Lucille Bell

Song: God Favored Me by Hezekiah Walker

Spirit Animal: Cat

Mystery Ingredient: Laughter

Sisterhood Ain't Easy, But It's Worth It

ear Sis,

God knew we needed each other. I knew the first day I met you that we would be the best of friends. We met each other, and we were both broken. It was the pain in your eyes that clung me to you. I felt the pain that I saw in you. I would like to think you chose me. You were very blunt and straightforward which was very different for me. I thought you were rude and ill mannered, but I liked you. I've had friendships before, but this friendship was "real." We hung out almost every day. Our friendship was very dysfunctional. You knew it, I knew it, and we did not care because it made sense to us.

It started off easy because we were young and careless. We had so much in common. We were both dysfunctional and lacked self-awareness. We cursed and yelled at each other. We cut each other off for long periods of time. I would have to admit I was more stubborn than you. Our first fight of many, we did not speak for a year. You moved to another state to follow your dreams, and you reached out to me. I was happy to have you back in my life because it felt right. At that time, we were still very young and ignorant. We had a disagreement, and you cut me off for a year. Time away from you was never easy. On the same token, there was no way I was going to apologize or kiss your behind. Needless to say, this was the beginning of our dysfunctional cycle. Whenever we reconnected, we discussed what happened but not how to move forward.

Life was hard, but with you by my side, it was better. Break ups from relationships, been there done that. Break ups from friendships, this was a different kind of pain. I would hurt in silence, but I wouldn't dare speak up about that. Life went on, and we both had to. Throughout the many years of our back and forth, we were growing as individuals. The time apart did us well. When we were apart, life happened. Shortly after I was pregnant with my daughter, I ended our friendship. This was very difficult for me. I'd met plenty of "acquaintances" after you, but the connection was not like ours. It was not familiar to me. Looking back, this was probably the time I needed you the most.

We spoke almost a year after me giving birth to my daughter. You, then, shared your good news about you expecting your daughter. I was excited for you and even more excited we would get the chance to experience motherhood together. We made a promise to put an end to our dysfunctional cycle.

We fell out again. However, instead of a year, it was two months that we did not speak. You suggested that we meet in person to resolve our conflict and settle our differences. This was probably one of the most uncomfortable conversations we have ever had. It wasn't easy, but it was worth it. We were both able to take accountability for our actions and move forward.

This time, I hope we move forward forever. We must take the painful lessons that we learned through sisterhood and equip our daughters with the ability to have sisterhood without the dysfunction. Sisterhood ain't easy, but it's worth it.

I love you …

Sierra Jackson
April 1989

About Sierra Jackson

Sierra believes mental health is a priority. She loves helping people, especially children. Sierra is a licensed psychotherapist and enjoys assisting her clients with their goals from beginning to end. She is compassionate and empathetic. Sierra volunteers as an advocate for children who are in foster care. She believes having the right support is essential in this life. She is a secretary of a non-profit organization that provides support to both teens and parents.

Moka, Teresa, R.

Black Girl Magic Recipe

Something Sweet: Pound Cake

Something Spicy: Jalapeños

Ancestor(s): Parents

Song: The Little Things by India Arie

Spirit Animal: Lioness

Mystery Ingredient: Prayer

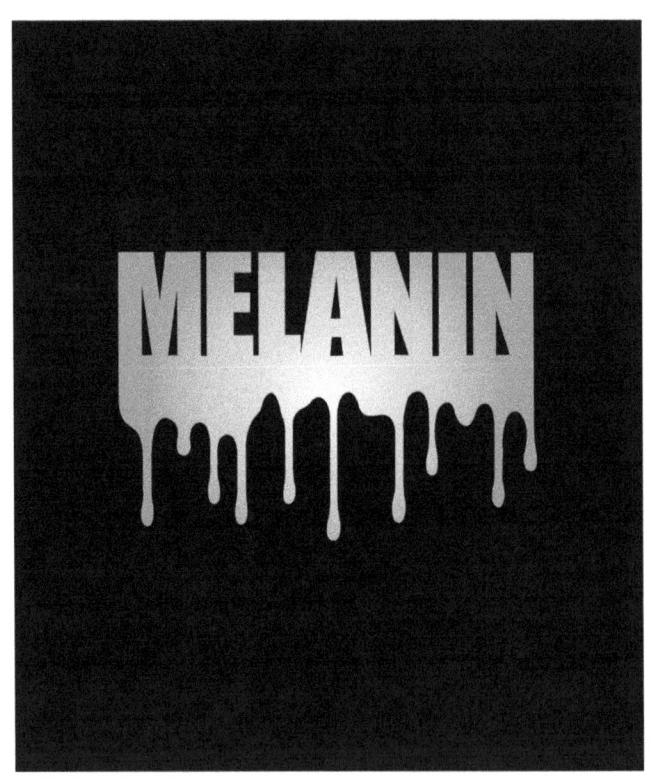

A Designer's Original

Dear Sis,

You are beautiful … fearfully and wonderfully made by the Supreme Creator! Know that you are a designer's original, and the world is waiting on you to show up! Get busy in the work of discovering YOUR life's true purpose because the world NEEDs you! I've learned that in order to do this, you will have to remove all distractions… distractions sometimes disguised as entertainment in the forms of Facebook, Netflix, YouTube. I'm not saying that these things are bad, but they can sometimes leave you with a distorted image of life and who you were meant to be. You must guard your spirit from the comparison of your life to someone else's social highlights and carefully constructed by images of 24/7 glamour and fun. The truth is that we are ALL spiritual beings having a human experience, and those experiences include a mixture of sunshine, rain, laughter, and tears. No one is up 24/7. So do not fall into the trap of believing that you are not enough, that you are not beautiful, or that you are missing out. Instead, tap into your true happiness, purpose, and peace that can be found by tuning into the divinity that is within you - the Holy Spirit. Dr. Myles Munroe reminded us that we look to the manufacturer of a product to seek answers about its design or purpose. Likewise, we must look to the "Great Manufacturer" when we have questions about our purpose and design. Only He can explain what you were created to do. As you ask these questions, it is important to be still and listen for the response. You may need to turn off the television and steal away to your place of solitude to hear what the "Great Manufacturer" is telling you. I will leave you with a tip that I has helped me along the way:

Bookend your day- Susan L. Taylor reminds us to give ourselves to ourselves before we give ourselves to the world. Each morning, begin your day with a ritual that centers you for your day. Spend time in meditation and communication with your Creator to gain clarity and direction. You may have to get up a little earlier to have that time, but you owe it to yourself to have that time before you enter the world. Likewise, end your day with a ritual that includes something pleasant each evening. It could be a bubble bath, a treat of some sort, or a good movie. Whatever it is, reward yourself with something pleasant each day. You are beautiful and divine…a designer's original. Don't sleep on that. Get up and be all that you were created to be!

I love you …

Teresa R. Moka
March 1982

About Teresa R. Moka

Teresa Moka is a devoted wife and mother who celebrates life, love, and laughter with family daily! Teresa is an 18-year veteran in the field of education. She works tirelessly to create a holistic educational environment that nurtures the whole child and ensures high levels of learning for all students. Teresa enjoys supporting and developing instructional capacity in educators and instructional leaders!

Nazare, Vernice

Black Girl Magic Recipe

Something Sweet: Peach Cobbler

Something Spicy: Bourbon Whiskey

Ancestor(s): Vernice and Nazare
(*my maternal and paternal great-grandmothers respectively, respectably, and lovingly*)

Songs:
Bigger by Beyonce | Black Girl Magik by Sampa the Great | Forever by Saroc
I Choose by India Arie

Spirit Animal: Chimpanzee

Mystery Ingredient: Curiosity

Friendship - The Long version

"A good friend knows all your stories. A best friend helped you write them."
-Author Unknown

This is the long version because the short version wasn't much shorter.

My longest and best friend relationship is with Erika.

We are both in our mid-forties now, but when we met in 6th grade, we actually *couldn't stand* each other. At least, I couldn't stand her. We were complete opposites. She was tall and light-skinned with curly and wavy hair always cut and styled from the salon. She wore the latest fashions tie dyed, stone-washed denim from the popular fashion lines, "Used" and "Damaged" (y'all don't know nothing about them "Used" & "Damaged") and Air Jordans. She also hung with the cool kids.

She'll tell you that she didn't like me because I thought I was all of that because I was the teacher's pet who kept getting picked to be the library helper which allowed me to leave class, and because I wouldn't let anyone copy off of my paper.

Before the year was out, I transferred to a 7th school for the 8th time. My mother, sister, and I were homeless again. We usually stayed with a family member, friend, or a neighbor if the women's shelter that accepted my mother didn't allow children. My younger sister was placed in remedial classes because she never stayed anywhere long enough to learn the lessons. We stayed with our grandma again, all the way through 7th grade. Then, grandma fell in love, got married, and downsized to a place with just enough room for her and her new husband.

There was no room for us there, besides my other aunts and my uncle came and stayed awhile and sometimes left their children too. Grandma was exhausted and frustrated from doing for everyone while still working. I can understand her wanting to enjoy her life. Besides, Bianca and I were tearing up her house. Bianca spilled red Kool-Aid on her white carpet. I forgot that I was running water for a bath and flooded her entire finished and furnished basement. One time I forgot about a pot on the stove and started a fire in the kitchen. Then, I wrapped a potato in aluminum foil and put it in the microwave. Microwaves were new, and I hadn't learned the difference yet. *"It's just like using an oven only faster,"* they said. Oh, and one time I was hanging with the girl from school and her mother had the police come to my grandmother's house with a search warrant to check my room looking for jewelry that was stolen from her house. Ooh, my grandmother was hot. I had the police coming into her house talking about stolen merchandise. I never told on my friend, but her mother soon found out that my friend used to sneak boys in, and they were the real culprits. Her mother only knew, or thought, that I was in the house. But it would be okay for me and Bianca because a neighbor, with whom we once lived, heard about our situation and allowed us to move back in with them again.

Let's call them the Generous family. Four generations living in a three-bedroom apartment, well, four bedrooms once they turned the pantry into a bedroom, and they still made room for me and my sister to sleep on the pull out couch. They shared what they had with us. Granny Generous and her Mister had the main bedroom. Granny's two sons, one still in high school and the other just graduated, shared one of the bedrooms. Granny also had two adult daughters, who each had two children. The two sisters each had their own room that they shared with their two children. The bedroom that was originally a pantry was large enough to fit a twin sized bed, that the three of them shared, and a tv. The other sister had two twin sized beds in her room. Her son slept in one of the beds, and she and her daughter shared the other bed.

I was always responsible for my sister. I woke her up and helped her get ready for school in the morning. I was responsible for combing her hair, walking her to and from school, making sure she brushed her teeth and did her homework, washing our clothes for the next day, and most importantly, making sure she stayed out of the way. I always felt like adults picked on Bianca because she was a curious and confident kid. I felt like they wanted her to sit quietly still in a chair with her hands folded for the whole day. They would complain or scold her if she asked a question, touched anything, laughed, or simply claimed her space to be a person. How are kids supposed to behave? Those experiences made Bianca and me close. We protected each other and our stuff. We didn't have our own space, our own room, or even dressers. Everything we had was in a bag that stayed neatly out of the way, out of sight.

Once we celebrated grandma and her new love, we moved and transferred back into the school at the beginning of the school year. My 8th grade teacher assigned seats, and Erika and I sat face to face. With side eyes, smacking lips, hard sighs, and heavy attitude I said, "Why do I have to sit in front of her?" The first moment I realized that Erika wasn't so bad was when we were trying to read the blackboard, and she asked what it read. Hell, I didn't know because I couldn't make out some of the letters either. "Is that a 's' or a 'n'. Maybe it's a 'e'?" Here we both were, squinting and using context clues with the other letters and words surrounding them, trying to figure out what this important word was. I was thinking, *How could her parents spend all this money on clothes and hair but wouldn't buy her glasses?* My mom already told me that we simply couldn't afford glasses.

The other time, I remember my heart softening towards Erika was on a day when I was wearing heavy clothes and a big coat. She asked me why I was dressed for cold weather when it was so hot outside. I explained that it took me 2.5 hours to get to school in the morning. My mom had gotten placed in permanent housing, and it was all the way on the other side of town. My mother wanted us to finish out the year in the same school, so we commuted by train for the next couple of months. I was being considered for the Salutatorian of my 8th grade class. In the morning, my mother walked my sister and me to the train somewhere between 5 and 6 am and it's always 10 or 20 degrees colder at that time of the morning than it was at noon. I had no idea that there could even be that big of a temperature change in one day. I was musty by lunch. That was how I learned to layer my clothes and always to carry deodorant in my bag. Erika chuckled and said, "Man, that's far. Y'all can stay with me. My mom won't care."

Speaking of Erika's mom, I imagined, by Erika's demeanor and how she was always styled, that her mom was Dianne Carroll or the Beyonce of our time. I imagined the house, family, the comforts, and the luxury for her "Cosby Show" style. Then, on report card day, when the parents had to pick up the report cards directly from the teacher, Ms. Shirley walked in short and round, wearing a red house dress, and red house shoes, with red hair freshly combed out from her roller set. Erika said, "That's my mom." I said, unbelievingly, "You lying. Quit playing." She assured me that she was for real. That's her mom. After accepting the report card and whatever critique the teacher shared about Erika, Ms. Shirley addressed Erika, "Come straight home." Ms. Shirley was no Dianna Carroll, no Beyonce, and no Phylicia Rashaad. That was the moment I considered that all of the students in our school were poor and underprivileged no matter how nicely they dressed. No one was there by choice but by circumstance.

Ms. Shirley was a lady who took Erika in when she was just 4 years old. Ms. Shirley was a friend of the man who Erika called her father, though she knew he was really not her biological father. Still, he had been looking out for her as long as she could remember. He spent time in and out of jail for dealing drugs. When he had money and was not locked up, he gave money and clothes to Erika and Ms. Shirley. He asked Ms Shirley if she would watch 4-year-old Erika for a few hours and didn't come back for days or weeks. I learned later that Erika's biological mother had a severe addiction and was barely able to care for herself, let alone a child. Ms. Shirley didn't have children of her own, but she treated Erika as such, providing, nurturing, and disciplining. She never pursued an actual adoption; she just stepped in and stepped up. Erika's real grandmother despised her daughter and passed that attitude on to Erika. Ms. Shirley told me that when she would send Erika there to visit, the grandmother would confiscate Erika's clothes, the clothes that Ms. Shirley had bought with her own money, claiming that they were too nice for Erika and that Erika didn't deserve them. The grandmother would give the clothes that Ms. Shirley bought and had packed for Erika, to a cousin. The grandmother would send Erika home to Ms. Shirley with the cousin's old clothes. Ms. Shirley said one time Erika showed up with a cigarette burn on her forehead. Ms. Shirley also let me see paper cards young Erika had made for her, thanking Ms. Shirley for feeding her.

Erika and I became and remained real friends. Many adventures ensued. I spent a lot of time at Erika's house. Ms. Shirley yelled and screamed at the both of us for being hot, fast, and disobedient. She threatened to bust our heads 'til the white meat showed. I thought she was going to pop a blood vessel. Erika assured me not to worry, Ms. Shirley always screamed like that. And she did. I remember helping Ms. Shirley wrap Christmas gifts, and when she ran low on money, she would buy two for a dollar pantyhose so that she would have a gift for everyone.

When my 16-year-old attitude didn't fit in my mother's house, I went to live with Erika for about two weeks until things smoothed over. I took my first ride on an airplane and my first trip to Florida going to visit Erika when she first joined the Navy. My second time on a plane was going to visit Erika while she was stationed in Nevada. We drove to Las Vegas, another first, and we both got our first tattoos. Erika was the first of my peers to buy a brand-new car and to buy a house. She found refuge from a dangerous relationship and traveled the world in the Navy. She also provided a life of adventure and experiences for the both of us. We both took care of Ms. Shirley. While Erika was in the Navy, I took Ms. Shirley to the grocery store and to her doctor's appointments, kept her hair that signature fire red color, and had many breakfasts with her where I learned more of the truth that shattered the story I had made up in my head about why I initially couldn't stand Erika. I wasn't trying to compete with Erika over whose life was harder. I'm just glad that we survived. I learned to be open to different sides of the story that I am telling myself. I learned about generosity. I learned about forgiveness and grace. I learned how a simple act of sharing, caring, and vulnerability can change the trajectory of another person's life. One time when I was really ready for a change, Erika even offered me the opportunity to live in her rental home when she was being reassigned. She said that I could just pay what I could until I recovered financially from the move.

Today

Erika has one daughter and is currently serving her 24th year as a Senior Chief officer in the Navy, an ordained minister, and a certified life coach. She serves as a counselor to members in the Navy. Erika plans to open a coffee shop with a theme for words, designed for community and conversation when she retires from the Navy.

Bianca won the regional Spelling Bee in the 6th grade and continued to excel on through school participating in multiple clubs and organizations. She graduated as the valedictorian of her high school class. She was awarded multiple scholarships including two full scholarships, one from the United Negro College Fund and the other from her alma mater, Spelman College. Bianca is married with one daughter and is a recruiter and a consultant for political candidates who want to see change in the world and their campaigns.

And me, well, I just do what I wanna do when I wanna do it. I consider myself a butterfly. I could finish my bachelor's degree in one year if I wanted to, but I'm a habitual student. I began my studies in engineering simply because I like math but switched my major to Sales and Marketing towards the end when I realized that my real interest was in the magic of how a 30 second commercial can influence people's buying decisions and their entire lives. I worked for Comcast Cable for 15 years and built a very comfortable life for myself all while dabbling in various side hustles including the beauty industry, insurance, real estate, gardening, etc. All those skills came together when I resigned from Comcast and moved to Arkansas to work with my father in his commercial construction painting business. I, too, am a certified life coach. And now I am combining all the skills and experiences that I have endured to create PlaceForResources.

PlaceForResources is a life skills course to help people, young and old, male and female, navigate life. Its purpose is to educate and expose people to the places, persons, things, and ideas that bring purpose, validation, and innovation to their lives aiding in their survival and the quality of their lives. It is the big brother, big sister information that I wish I had when I was growing up.

We all still got each other's backs and are full blown support systems for each other. What you need? I got you! I'm on my way…

I love you …

Vernice Nazare
November 1977

About Vernice Nazare

Vernice Nazare often refers to herself as a butterfly. She's a pollinator - sharing resources, information, and connecting, all the nouns to nurture our communities to be stronger, healthier, and more vibrant.

Her work balances between the entrepreneurial and community arena. She is the founder of a PlaceForResources which is a hub for professional and personal growth courses for young women with a focus on business, confidence, and self-sufficiency skills.

Vernice has studied and practiced in multiple industries. She has combined her studies of engineering, marketing and ecommerce. She has also worked in insurance & mortgage loan origination. She has certifications from SBA's Emerging Leaders and Abundant Life Path University.

She volunteers for initiatives that focus on urban community gardens and conservation, pregnant and parenting teens, and the homeless community.

Neal, Andrea L.

Black Girl Magic Recipe

Something Sweet: Watermelon

Something Spicy: A sexy man in the sun

Ancestor(s): Lois Roddy

Song: Wipe Me Down, by Boosie Badazz

Spirit Animal: A Serpent

Mystery Ingredient: Persistence

keep going

A Few Things I've Learned

ear Sis,

I read the writing prompts for this assignment, and like most things in my life, I could not choose just one topic to discuss. I've decided to pick a few where I will briefly share a few things I've learned that I wish I had learned sooner and a few things I hope you will use as tools to help you navigate life and sisterhood.

Toward the end of 2019, I decided to be intentional with my effort toward sisterhood. I put my intentions out into the multiverse and had no idea of the journey that 2020 and 2021 would bring. Many of these messages did not come packaged in colorful, one- or two-line Hallmark messages. However, some were given like the comfort on a comfortable bed after a hard day in this world. There were mirrors that appeared that showed me that I needed to extend the very attributes I needed to receive for myself. For example, I needed to become a better listener and a verbal cheerleader. There are women who I am deeply in awe of, and I never knew how to articulate how I see them. Now, I randomly send messages simply saying they are a dope person or something specifically that they do that inspires me. On social media, emoji's have done the job when I don't have the words. This extends to people in my intimate circle and people who I only interact with on social media. While I actively listen and try to be a lending ear to those who reach out to me for support, I realize that I do not always need to insert my thoughts and perspective into the conversation. I listen and ask questions to make sure I understand what my sister is saying and to ensure that she feel heard. Please know that this is not something I woke up achieving. This takes work and intention on my end.

However, I noticed that I also needed to advocate for myself and create boundaries. I no longer would allow people to say and treat me any type of way because they have been in my life for a certain period of time, or they excelled in certain areas of their lives. I set boundaries and if people didn't treat me how I wanted to be treated, they were either fully removed from my life, or access was limited. This was hard most times and done in frustration other times, but now I am to the point where I can firmly yet gracefully maneuver this practice. It's freeing and securing. Every day we have to fight something either for ourselves or for the world, and I refuse to do the same in my inner circle. I used to think that this was arrogant or rigid behavior when I saw others do this. Now, I realize that its literally sanity and self-preservation. People are always going to choose themselves even if it's at your detriment, and if you aren't protecting yourself, then you are going to get used up and told it's your fault for allowing people to abuse you. Unfortunately, this world does not protect Black girls or women. I used to think that this mindset was rooted in bitterness, but I now realize that not accepting this as reality and using it as a tool of life is unwise. Now, this doesn't mean to get people before they get you. No, this means to give after you take care of yourself.

Black women have so many things in common and attributes that unite us. However, I learned that we are all still people from various backgrounds with unique lived experiences. Personalities will sometimes clash and that doesn't mean that someone is a bad person. However, that can mean that those people may not need to have immediate or intimate access to you. It is totally okay to cheer from the sideline and go home. Unfortunately, due to slavery and centuries of oppression, we are taught to compete and resent each other. There are people who look like you who feel that they are genuinely supporting you, but there is an internal conflict they may not even be aware of that causes them to hinder your growth, resent your movement or successes, or not to want your light to shine too bright. Instead of spending time trying to navigate through their issues, utilize that time to work on yourself, not exhibit these behaviors to other sisters, and continue to move forward.

The past years have brought me other Black women who have expanded my mind and contributed to both my spiritual growth and professional progression. I realized that while I fully understood my purpose there was something lacking. I began to look at women famous, not so famous, and everywhere in between whom I admire. I realized that they either have found a place of peace and freedom or are striving to achieve these positions. I have now set out to maintain a peaceful existence and to seek freedom in all areas of my life. Self-care is presented as a 1-2-3 format. A group of people who have historically been utilized as mules and servants, have to first learn who they are, what they want, and how to care for themselves while fighting oppression, dismantling stereotypes, and not feeling guilty for putting themselves first. There is not a simple solution to obtain this level of self-awareness and enforcement of boundaries. Therapy isn't attainable for all, and when it is, how do you even find a person who has the cultural knowledge and compatibility to assist you in unpacking all of your challenges? The space for self is limited when over half of us are in survival mode financially, with family and trauma.

I realized the social power that we have after this election. We are always heard when our voices, style, or souls can be capitalized. So, what if we use that energy and power to allow the space for our sisters to care for ourselves? This will look different for each individual person. Sometimes it's the ear that we need, but it could also be the resource that we need. It could be taking the information that a sister tells us to the seat of power that we have to initiate change. It could also be listening to the constructive criticism that we don't want to hear, and making ourselves, our business, and our families better and stronger.

I noticed that Black women have always been defiant in the acts of patriarchy, our voices, our hair, our style, our cooking, and so on. I feel that we have felt unheard and powerless for so long that we are now attempting to utilize the areas where we are criticized to "act out" versus to stand in defiance. We don't have to succumb to tricks and degradation for respect and attention. Just being…ourselves, intelligent, creative, and different are all the methods that we need to keep them feeling insecure and bankrupt attempting to be us.

I want to leave you with the words of my late Aunt Marie. There are two things in this world that are finite … time and love. Use your time wisely and love and receive as much love as you possibly can before you leave this place. The only things that matter when you are gone is who you did or did not spend time with and if the people you left know that you loved them and that you know that you were loved.

I love you …

Andrea L Neal
May 1983

About Andrea L. Neal

Andrea L. Neal is currently the Director of Compliance Equity at Maryland Institute for Creative Arts (MICA). MICA is an internationally known, highly regarded art school located in Baltimore, Maryland. In this inaugural role, Andrea provides training centered around sex discrimination and misconduct, biases, and equity. She also serves as the college's Title IX Coordinator where she ensures that the campus is in compliance with federal regulations and investigations and that complaints are resolved fairly.

Prior to working at MICA, she worked as the Deputy Title IX Coordinator at Goucher College, a four-year private liberal arts college also located in Baltimore, MD. As the Title IX/ADA Coordinator at the University of Arkansas for Medical Sciences (UAMS), she oversaw allegations, policy, procedures related to sex misconduct and provided accommodations to students with disabilities. Andrea transitioned to this role from Arkansas Baptist College, where she was the ADA Coordinator at Arkansas Baptist College, a four-year liberal arts historically Black college located in Little Rock, Arkansas. Andrea is the co-chair for the Racial and Ethnic Diversity and Disability Special Interest Group (REDD SIG) for the Association on Higher Education and Disability (AHEAD). AHEAD is a national association for individuals committed to equity for persons with disabilities in higher education. She serves as the Immediate Past President of Ark-AHEAD, which is the Arkansas affiliate to AHEAD. Andrea has served as the Diversity, Equity, and Inclusion committee chair for the PeaceKeepers, where she assists with fundraising and support for Women's and Children's First, one of the oldest domestic violence shelters in the state of Arkansas.

Andrea L. Neal is a native of Little Rock, Arkansas, where she graduated from the historic Little Rock Central High, and the University of Arkansas, Little Rock. She relocated to Dallas, Texas from 2006 to 2014 where she grew personally and professionally. She relocated back to Little Rock, purchased the house across the street from her childhood home, and assisted with revitalizing the area by renovating houses.

OKEKE, NGOZIKA

Black Girl Magic

Something Sweet: Moscato

Something Spicy: Cayenne pepper

Ancestor(s): Bell Hooks

Song: Take Over Control, by Afrojack feat. Eva Simons

Spirit Animal/Person(s): Eartha Kitt

Mystery Ingredient: Grapefruit and Mint

All That We Are

ear Sis,

You are all that you were created to be.

/

/Being all that I am

/Lends to all that we are

/The Collective

/Resilient

/The Genesis, representing a type of beauty that words couldn't quantify; before beauty ever was

/Bonds that can't be broken

/Mirroring the women that were before us

/Not monolith

/Not angry

/Not strong like they say…

/But strong like we are

/Delicate like bombs that shower a world in awe of their glory AND their wrath

/An amalgamation of all the things that we are because we had to be

/Now we can select-

/…ALL, SOME, or NONE of the identities that we were once relegated to because we're

/Dripping in gold

/Oozing confidence even with clipped wings

/So, it seems…

/The spirit may be broken

/But in Us

/The outward expression of who we are always shines through

/The lull of greatness is echoed in everything that we do

/Not monolith

/Not angry

/Not strong like they say

/But strong like we are

/Delicate like bombs that shower a world in awe of their glory AND their wrath

/An amalgamation of all the things that we are because we had to be

/A still, small chorus of voices from those of the past that beat along the same drums that we play today

/But they say

/That the bond we have can't be authentic-

/That we must be pitted against each other; but if so, then who suffers?

/Not them, but us

/It's got to be enough…

/To know that together we can be…

/Any and all things wrapped up in the glory of what could have once been described as unfathomable

/The uniqueness in us proclaims once again that we are many things, but we are-

/Not monolith

/Not angry

/Not strong like they say

/But strong like we are

/Delicate like bombs that shower a world in awe of their glory AND their wrath

/An amalgamation of all the things that we are because we had to be

/And to me

/There's no end to what we can and already possess

/It's full circle; all included

/Resilient

/The Collective

/Being who I am

/Lends to all that we are

/

I love you …

Ngozika Okeke
August 1988

About Ngozika Okeke

Ngozika O'keke is a marketing consultant turned socially conscious fashion designer now based in Los Angeles, CA. Following graduate school & consulting for private sector firms, it was the decision to re-brand the clothing line and relocate that changed the course of her career. The eponymous brand now has a cause. With ties to local charitable organizations, Ngozika O'keke Clothing now proudly donates a portion of all revenue to organizations that work with survivors of sexual assault and domestic abuse. Marrying the idea of fashion and philanthropy is what landed Ngozika the opportunity to compete on Season 3 of an international design reality show "Design Genius" of Fashion One Network and Netflix series "Pet Stars."

When asked about the brand she is building, Ngozika simply states that the idea is to bring awareness, to aid in prevention of assault and also to make people look and feel fabulous while helping to improve the human experience.

Olamide', Jionni

Black Girl Magic Recipe

Something Sweet: Mama's Holiday Brownies

Something Spicy: Nawlin's Crawfish

Ancestor(s): Addie Mae Carr

Song: Harder than my Demons by Big Sean

Spirit Animal: Hawk's Eye

Mystery Ingredient: Truth and Love with a lil Bih (*don't play with me*)

To Infinity and Beyond

Dear Sis,

We are children of infinity,

Birthed in the triple darkness of the Black womb.

Black bodies are all kin to me

Shared consciousness all in my memory.

Stories from my grandmothers who said, "sit with me."

Never met them, but they taught me through energy

Reminding me they're always in the inner me.

They said, "Sit with me and hear my story,

Need you to run back and tell that for me.

Don't let them take your crown or your glory.

Let your assignment flow to you, no need for forcing it.

Don't give more than your due apportionment."

Thank You, Creator for the struggles."

Thank You for the triumphs.

Thank You for the reminders that we stand on the shoulders of many giants.

Thank You for the long nights and the quiet mornings.

Thank You for the valley lows and flights with the eagles soaring.

Thank You for the medicine in the grass and the wind, the rivers and the trees.

I'm thankful for the blessings coming to you because they're in proximity to me.

I give thanks for all the love that comes because it's free.

Grateful to come from the eternal darkness, the black matter of infinity.

I am Vaseline, shea butter, Oil of Olay.

I am herb medicine, sweet grass, and peyote.

I am Summer's Eve and *Poetic Justice*.

I'm a fiery night and wanderlust.

We make medicine and make magic.

We usher in peace, and we wreak havoc.

Transition of the age, now the healers have it

To civilize the mind away from moving like a savage.

Grateful for all my mama's teachings,

whether she loved me whole, or she was absentee.

Just like a moon go crescent, missing the greatest part of itself,

It still serves a purpose in the sky that only it can for all the world to see.

Never to be erased, unable to be denied,

Black life is the source of creation.

In the woman is always Black pride.

That's my Black mama, Black woman to the world.

Sacred as an elder and sacred as a little girl,

Sacred in our faces and sacred in our names,

may our women inherit the earth.

May we witness the world change.

I love you …

Jionni Olamide'
October 1988

About Jionni Olamide'

Jionni is your <u>Spiritual Plug</u>. She is a radical truth teller promoting healing, liberation, and creation.

When you share space with Jionni, you are going to be immersed in self-improvement, self-love, and self-appreciation. She pours into the community with spiritual guidance, Healing Circles, youth programs, Community Gardens, and building Self Sustaining Communities.

Jionni created <u>The Alternative Tribe</u> to build structures that afford members the freedom to heal and be whole. The vision is to grow and sustain a village that autonomously self-governs its own reality and future through acquiring education, land, skills, resources, and infrastructure through community development.

Jionni is the author of <u>A Secret Pack of Passages: Transforming Pain into Purpose</u> and the artist of the woman empowerment song, <u>World Changes</u>.

Pendelton, Jacqueline

Black Girl Magic Recipe

Something Sweet: Aunt Shirley's Caramel Cake

Something Spicy: Good 'ole Louisiana Hot Sauce on most soul foods!

Ancestor(s): Bessie Cade Washington

Song: Beautiful Skin by Goodie Mob

Spirit Animal: Female Lion

Mystery Ingredient: Just one?
Laughter, Honesty, and Loyalty

Enjoy the Small Things

Aunt Shirley's Caramel Cake:

<u>**Cake:**</u> Use the Duncan Hines Butter Cake Mix – Follow instructions on the box

<u>Caramel Ingredients:</u>

- ❖ 1 can of Pet milk or Carnation Milk
- ❖ 1 cup of sugar
- ❖ 1 stick of butter
- ❖ 1 teaspoon of vanilla extract

<u>Instructions:</u>

- ❖ Stir over medium heat consistently for 45 mins to an hour until it has reached a silky brown caramel consistency. Take a seat and listen to some good tunes as you must not leave it unattended until consistency is reached.
- ❖ Poke a few holes in top of the already cool baked cake and pour caramel over the cake to enjoy a taste of heaven in every bite.

ear Sis,

The previous cake recipe is one of my favorite baked recipes passed down from an aunt of mine. Growing up, Christmas afternoon was always celebrated at Big Momma's house (maternal Grandmother) where fellowship was always centered around food and laughter. Each aunt (10 girls – 16 kids total) had a special dish she would bring, and we could not proceed with prayer and breaking of bread until they all were present. Aunt Shirley's was the Caramel Cake! The only desert you needed, most times it would be cut and devoured within 5 mins from the conclusion of prayer. If you don't know, you betta ask somebody! It felt as though all was well with the world when we were living in those moments.

This recipe, much like many others passed down in my family, reminds me of life. It doesn't take much to satisfy the human soul, and far too often, we tend to lose sight of the most gratifying things in life, due to succumbing to the many oppressions the world places on us (BLACK FOLK). This very simple recipe unfolds so many beautiful memories, conversations, and lessons to take along this journey in life.

I am not at all a cook; in fact, I am a proud head member of the cleanup crew! Though, I certainly have a pallet for the many savory delicacies our culture has to offer the world along with their origin and most importantly grateful for the lessons learned while basking in presence of preparation. If you take nothing from this passage, I ask that you take a beat and ENJOY THE SMALL THINGS, for it's the small things that bring us fulfillment and pleasure!

I love you …

Jacqueline Pendleton
November 1986

About Jacqueline Pendleton

Jacqueline Pendleton is a Little Rock, Arkansas native and a University of Arkansas at Little Rock (UALR) graduate with a Bachelor of Health Sciences/Community Health Promotions and a Master of Public Health from Grand Canyon University. She has over 12 years of experience in the field of healthcare and is currently a Regional Compliance Professional for a Fortune 500 health insurance company. She is also Founder/CEO of Respectfully Social, an organization curated for women of color in the state of Arkansas, to have an outlet that allows them to be their authentic selves in a safe place.

Her interest has always been to make significant contributions in a public health environment by assisting those in need, particularly minorities. Henceforth, in her current position, she works actively to assist those, who desire, to improve health disparities within the community for the better. Pouring back into her community is something she is fond of while she does so as an active member of Junior League as well as volunteering her time to the Alzheimer's Association as an executive leader.

She is also a loving daughter, sister, aunt, wife, and soon to be mother who absolutely loves to travel, expand her pallet with all the cultural delicacies, sip wine while pouring into her "Girls," and loving her family!

Pettway LAC, Isis J.

Black Girl Magic Recipe

Something Sweet: Tea cakes

Something Spicy: Gumbo

Ancestor(s): Theodis Jones

Song: Soar by Christina Aguilera

Spirit Animal: Butterfly

Mystery Ingredient: Poetry

When Time Marches on and the New Arguments That Come Along with It

Dear Sis,

A mirror is an important item in a household. It is used in assisting people to get up and get ready for the day ahead of them. Mirrors also allow us to look at the reflection of ourselves. Sometimes, we can look into a mirror and see ourselves without seeing ourselves, which is why I was excited, in April of 2016, when Beyoncé released her much awaited sixth album *Lemonade*. Unlike any of her previous work, Beyoncé gave her audience beautiful poetry, courtesy of Warsane Shire, and images upon images of the southern culture of Black women. It was amazing to watch because representation matters. In a society that has defined me by the caricatures of Jezebel, Mammy, and Sapphire, Beyoncé's *Lemonade* was as refreshing as the drink on a hot summer's day. *Lemonade* allowed me to see a woman, a Black woman, who was hurting, angry, in love, carefree, strong, and more in an unapologetic manner. *Lemonade* showed me I still have much to learn and even more to unlearn along the way. *Lemonade* also featured Beyonce surrounded by other Black women and showcased the importance of sisterhoods among us.

Black women and sisterhoods go together like peanut butter and jelly. Our sisterhoods hold us up and are a part of sustaining us through the good and bad times in our lives. Therefore, the older I get the more I understand the importance of these connections. My understanding of sisterhood has changed throughout the years, and I am grateful for growth. This journey to understanding the importance of sisterhood became more in depth once I stopped centering men in my life. You see I grew up around purity culture, in a Black Baptist church that taught/groomed me to be a wife before being a full human being. Therefore, friendships were fine but were not on the same level as romantic companionship, at least that's what I grew up believing in my youth and during my 20s. Ha! In the words of Julia Roberts in *Pretty Woman*, "Big mistake. HUGE!" The journey in understanding sisterhood has come with acknowledgment of understanding that people change, uncomfortable conversations are necessary, and sometimes new agreements have to be made to accommodate the growth in these circles.

Throughout my life, I've made connections with people who have become friends, mentors, etc. With establishing sisterhood circles, some have been intentional and some by accident. During my Atlanta years, I met a beautiful group of older Black women who took me under their wing. These women were a huge part of my growth in my 20s and even when I gave birth to my son. They are one sisterhood circle in my life. My very first sisterhood circle can be traced back to elementary and junior high school years. Then, others I established during the various transitions in my life. Now one thing to understand about sisterhood circles, through the years, is that becoming adults will test them. During adulthood our careers are taking off, kids are born, people are getting married, moving, caretaking, etc. I had to dig deep to understand the changes and not take it personally as I hope no one took my absences personally. I had to stop expecting myself from others and free myself from that mental prison. I also found that, in sisterhood, sometimes new agreements have to be made,

And that's ok!

I love you ...

Isis J. Pettway, LAC
February 1982

About Isis J. Pettaway

A calm, creative, and compassionate person who continues to take up space with her personal and professional growth, Isis Pettway is a licensed mental health therapist serving residents in the state of AR. As a mental health professional, she desires to continue the work of shattering the stigma around mental health. When she's not working, volunteering, and/or shopping for new books, she's spending time with family and friends.

Richardson, Casey Ariel

Black Girl Magic Recipe

Something Sweet: Amaretto Sour

Something Spicy: Your Favorite Auntie

Ancestor(s): Maya Angelou

Song: Ava by Pip Millett

Spirit Animal: Lion

Mystery Ingredient: Megan Thee Stallion Knees

All the Things I Couldn't Say

"Well, if I make you feel the way that you say I do – why are we friends?!"

"I'm not going anywhere."

"Why?"

"Because I love you."

I held my phone … looking at the group text message thread. Though I was fuming, I didn't know how to reply to a message like that. What *could* be a reply to that? I was completely stumped.

As I sat balled up on my bed – back to my headboard and knees to my chest – tears began to sting my eyes. My frustration grew, in large part, because I didn't know how to process what I was feeling. I didn't want to. Whatever was going on with me was stupid … but not unfamiliar.

I didn't text back to say that I was starting to cry. I didn't text that I loved her too. I didn't explain that I was having a hard time processing my emotions in that moment. I didn't say anything. For a full 24 hours, I didn't say anything.

Protection was the only language that I was fluent in within my friendships. I was not familiar with soft caresses, nor the long, warm hugs that are filled with smells of sweet perfume, the kind that makes your eyes close and lips curl. Those incredibly soft hugs that rock you back and forth, making you feel suspended in time, safe and grounded,

I was a warrior. I was a protector of fragile beings, rational above all else, and numb to the things that might cause my frail humanity to lead the way. People needed me to be strong for them, to help them transcend their problems, and to trample on the things in their lives that threatened to damage them. Or perhaps, I needed that. Perhaps, I was trying to save myself.

In truth, I was crippling at times. Throughout my life, I'd counted the collateral damage I caused as the price of being a truth bearer. I had such high standards for everything. I expected the very best out of everyone – from their character to their rationalization in decision-making. It was not uncommon for me to give blank stares when people had the audacity to make whimsical decisions for the hell of it, even when it was like they were touching a hot stove twice.

Perhaps, these standards were my way of keeping people at a comfortable distance. Perhaps, they were my way of assessing whether surrendering to intimacy in friendships was worth the risk of heartbreak in the end. Perhaps, I had a horrible tendency of skewing every outcome to a horrible extreme given my damaging childhood experiences – especially as they related to women.

I didn't know how to give what I had never held with both hands. I didn't know how to be happy with the present. I didn't know what it felt like not to be running from something. I didn't know how it felt to be satiated by what was already in my life, to stand still and commit myself fully to the things that were right in front of me.

Love. Safety. Sisterhood.

I now understand that I couldn't offer what I didn't understand myself. Vulnerability. I didn't want to risk the annihilation that might come from my exhaling and being penetrable. I'd already lost too much. I already carried around too much pain. To be pierced again, even at such a young age, might cause a blow from which I would never recover. I couldn't stand to lose the only thing I thought I owned – my will to fight.

At 31, I moved to Africa for a chance at complete liberation. I wanted deeply to exhale and lay every burden down. I went to spread my wings wider than I ever had before … to be lighter than I could have ever dreamed. I went after a chance to be reborn while there was still breath in my body, to heal my views of what the world could be, to sweeten the deal on what my life could be.

After spending time doing much-needed inner work, I was finally able to gaze outward and see that there is so much love in the world. There is so much space for me simply to be. In my brokenness, there is space for me. In my naivete, there is so much space for me. In my desire to be passionately loved, there is so much space for me. In my creative brilliance, there is so much space for me.

That space comes in the form of people opening arms wide to love me unconditionally. It comes in the form of strangers met along the journey who deposit the very things I need in my life at the exact time I need it. It comes in the form of tender, sweet lovemaking and the wiping of tears. It comes in the form of forehead kisses and backrubs. It comes in the form of people affirming me and honoring my innate gifts.

Having experienced the enormity of love that is in the world for me, I better understand the depth of love that my sisters deserve from me.

I'm learning to forgive myself every day for not being able to offer more to the people that I've loved along the journey to my current state. I'm learning to love more passionately today and to say all the things that I feel in the moment.

In this moment, the Casey of today will speak to the sister who responded all those years back with, "Because, I love you." I can't take back time, and I wouldn't change a thing if I could – as the events of my life have led me to where I now stand. Today, I'm better equipped to offer these flowers from an untainted lens.

Dear Sis,

Today, I know to tell you that you are beautiful … just the way that you are, that you have more courage than I could have ever dreamed of mustering up in the first 30 years of my life – the courage of not giving a damn about what the rules are.

Today, I know to tell you that your spirit of adventure is purer than anything I can understand – and it must be protected at all costs. You move the culture forward. My lack of understanding your dreams should never be a reason not to give it your all – and nor should anyone else's.

I now know to tell you that it is okay to make mistakes, that I trust you to love yourself enough always to walk towards the path that lifts you higher, and that you should trust yourself too. Every experience along your path will cause your heart, understanding and perspective to swell in beautiful ways.

I know to tell you that I am so very proud of you, sister, that you are the greatest thing in the world – simply because you are, and that God did a marvelous thing in creating you. I'm honored to know you, and I'm deeply blessed to have you in my life. Even if we cease to walk together as closely as we do now, you have left a life-long impression on my life that has changed me for the better.

I know to tell you that I appreciate every sacrifice you've made for me. Thank you for every dollar spent on flights to make sure that I was okay, every painful conversation you suffered through, just so I knew you wouldn't abandon me, every word you swallowed so that I would feel supported when I was taking huge, risky leaps, and every wrong you've forgiven because you understand the frailty of the human condition and my attempt at doing the very best I knew how.

I know to tell you that I'm always cheering you on – no matter the distance, that I'm always lifting you up in prayer and intentions, that you have risen past other people's expectations for your life, and that your entire existence is ministry.

Today, I know to tell you that:
I love you …

Casey Richardson
February 1990

About Casey A. Richardson

Casey Ariel Richardson is a published author, tech founder, and business coach to Black female entrepreneurs. She is the author of <u>Pain Unseen: The Truths That Lie Beneath My Strength</u>, a beautifully raw memoir that aims to break the cycle of silent suffering. To date, Casey's company BLAZE GROUP LLC has provided more than 3,500 Black female entrepreneurs with access to knowledge, capital, and mentorship. Casey is also the creator of a socio-business app for Black women, TablexTribe by BLAZE GROUP. Casey was honored for Best in Business & Finance in the 26th Annual Webby Awards, has spoken to companies and colleges around the globe, and has structured a first-of-its-kind pay-as-you-go tractor financing solution in Sub-Saharan Africa.

Sims, Nefatari

Black Girl Magic Recipe

Something Sweet: Pound cake (*from scratch*)

Something Spicy: Salsa

Ancestor(s): Sadie Franks (my granny)

Song: Lean on Me by Club Nouveau

Spirit Animal: Black Panther

Mystery Ingredient: Witty Sarcasm & BLING

Sisterhood

Dear Sis,

Sisterhood is defined as an association, society, or community of women linked by a common interest, religion, or trade. For most of us, sisterhood began in the home if we are fortunate of enough share parents with another female(s). Another form of sisterhood I am blessed to be a part of is a sorority. But, like family, a sorority affords you a multitude of sisters that you may or may not like. You can't choose your family, and you can always choose your sorority sisters. Then, there are women who become a part of your life. You couldn't have imagined, planned, predicted, or created a sister who would become part of the foundation you use to navigate the ups and downs of life.

Being born a Black woman affords you an automatic membership into Black sisterhood. This membership is experienced and expressed when you see another Black woman or group of Black women, and you feel the connection that is passed down to us from the strong women who came before us. While I love all my siblings, my relationship with my sister is different than with my brothers even though she is eleven years my junior. There were/are things we just get about each other. This is the beginning of my Black sisterhood. The bond that women, especially Black women, share is beautiful, deep, and magical.

We know what it means when a "sista" looks at us from head to toe and gives a wink or "that" smile that says, 'Yes, girl! I see you!" Black sisterhood is standing in the gap for the sister you don't even know in the grocery store or giving a sister an honest opinion when she's shopping alone and not sure about that outfit, even if it means telling her, "Not that color. Let's find something that works with your complexion." Black sisterhood means not letting your sister walk down the hall with toilet tissue on her shoe. It means being a shoulder to cry on when there are no words that will provide comfort. It means talking your sister down off the ledge when she's about to do something stupid as well as jumping off the ledge with her when necessary!

For me, outside of faith in my Lord and Savior, Jesus Christ and family, my sisters are completely necessary for me to endure the ups and downs of life. Most women navigate to some type of organization of mostly, if not all, women to fulfill some type of need in life. It may be a church or a service organization. We also have a smaller core group of women, typically three to five who serve as our sounding boards, prayer partners, partners in crime, sense of reason to stop you from committing a crime (LOL), and hype woman. These ladies are your biggest cheerleaders and supporters. They will cry with you, laugh with you, keep your secrets, and check you when you need to be checked. A real true sister is as necessary as air if we are to be successful in life.

Becoming a member of Alpha Kappa Alpha Sorority Inc. strengthened my sisterhood experience. It felt like being wrapped in a blanket of love having women with common interests and goals in most any place I could travel in the world. This is how I met some of the women in my inner circle. The inner circle of Black sisterhood is like a hug from your mom or grandmother. The larger Black sisterhood experience is like that blanket I mentioned earlier. I have so many memories beginning in college that involve my sorority sisters. One that comes to mind and is the epitome my sisterhood experience happened on a trip to one of our conferences. I was in college, and we had chartered a bus to travel to the city in which the conference was being held. We had a great time and were preparing to head back home. The bus had parked in the back of the hotel at the bottom of a grassy hill. We could have used the sidewalk, but it would have taken longer. I chose to go down the grassy hill directly to the bus. I took one step and slid all the way down the hill in my white pants! Everyone was standing there and saw me slip-slide my way to the bus. I came to a stop right in front of the door of the bus. Thankfully, nothing was hurt except my pride. So, I got up, brushed myself off as if nothing happened, and got on the bus. All my sorority sisters rushed to the bus and made sure I was okay. Once it was established that I was okay and the only fatality was my white pants (major grass stains), there was about 30 seconds of silence; then, the bus erupted in laughter, including me. This sums up sisterhood for me. They just saw me slide down that hill. Yet, they did not hesitate to rush down the same hill to come to my aid. Once they made sure I was okay, they released the laughter that was inevitably coming but held in until my safety was secured. They supported me when I needed it and laughed at me because it was funny!

I was traveling with a group of sister-friends and there was a plan to attend an event on day two of the trip. I connected with a couple of friends in the city we were in prior to said event. During that time, it started pouring down raining to the point that we had to wait it out, and my phone died. I couldn't communicate with the group I travelled with, and they were waiting on me because I was in the vehicle we were using. The others in my group were able to make it to the event we all were supposed to attend. I just happened to be nearby, and they saw me. It appeared to them that I had blown them off for the friends with whom I had met. Of course, they were livid! They tried to brush it off for the rest of the trip, but finally, they had to say something. They, clearly but respectfully, expressed their anger. I explained what happened on my end, and all was resolved. This taught me a few things. One, communication is key. In this instance, I couldn't communicate in the moment but should have made them aware of what happened immediately. Two, they should not have tried to brush their feelings under the rug. We wasted a day of this trip moving around in tension thick enough to cut. Once we all expressed our feelings and explained what happened, all was well, and the remainder of the trip was great. We laugh about it now, but that was a real moment. We became closer because of that moment of tension. We built a connection that allows us to share our feelings with each other even when it's not pleasant. There is safety in being vulnerable with your sister when you know the love is genuine.

There are occasions when sisterhood doesn't live up to what we imagine or expect. I strive to be the one my sisters/family can count on. If you need me, I'm there. It doesn't matter the time of day or night. If I have it, you have it. I will defend your honor in or out of your presence. I am the keeper of your secrets. I will also have the hard conversations and tell you the things you need to hear but may not want to. With that being said, a good sister is someone who does all of that but allows their sister(s) to do that for them as well. It is not fair to your sisters when you don't allow them to be there for you when you're in need. I am guilty of that. I'm so used to being the one who is the listening ear and standing in the gap when needed. It's not easy for me to ask for help, and we should not expect our sisters to know automatically we need help, although, most times they do know. In my case, my inner circle of sisters did know and approached me in love to let me know they noticed I was off, and they were there to help me. We had the discussion. I shared what I was going through, and they were there to help me. I needed them and didn't tell them. That was unfair to them and detrimental to me. I prolonged something that may have been over sooner, or at the very least, easier to deal with because I didn't share with my sisters. They loved me through it and later, read me my rights for not letting them in sooner, as they should have. That's what a sister does. When she knows you need a good talking to but can't handle it in the moment, she waits. She doesn't overload you, but she does let you know how she's feeling. I believe moments of conflict can strengthen any relationship if handled correctly.

Moments of conflict can strengthen relationships, but they can also end them. It's hard to let go of a friendship that has spanned decades, but sometimes it's necessary. Being a sister does not mean remaining in a relationship that causes harm to you physically or emotionally over a long period of time. If you've constantly been the sounding board and a voice of reason for this friend while not getting anything in return, you may want to evaluate whether the relationship is serving you and communicate that to your sister. If you communicate your feelings to your sister and she turns the tables by blaming you instead of listening to your concerns, RUN! I'm a firm believer that no relationship is in the position it is in (good, bad, or ugly) by the fault of one person. Each person bears some responsibility whether it's 90% vs 10% or 50% vs 50%. You don't owe your mental, physical, or emotional health to your sister. She is supposed to be there to help you through the valleys and celebrate on the mountain tops, not push you into the valley.

The next generation is in a prime position to build a strong sisterhood much earlier in life. While I believe in Black sisterhood, there is a dark side of that sisterhood exhibited by competitiveness, jealousy, and greed. I hope we can learn that if we work together, we all win and move away from the crabs in a barrel mentality. The mom from the movie "Soul Food" said it best. Individually, we can accomplish/withstand many things, but when we come together, we are a force to be reckoned with. Not many things are stronger than a Black woman. Very few things are stronger than a group of Black women.

   I love you …

Nefertari Sims
March 1971

About Nefertari Sims

Nefertari Sims. is a daughter, sister, and friend, but her most prized title is Auntie to the best Lil Bits (nieces and nephews) in the universe. She is a Senior Professional Business Analyst at DXC Technology. Nefertari earned a Bachelor of Business Administration with emphasis in Information Systems from the University of Central Arkansas and a Master of Arts in Computer Resources and Information Management from Webster University. She is passionate about working with other survivors of sexual abuse through her church and providing community service with her sorority. She loves spending time with her family and traveling.

Steward, April

Black Girl Magic Recipe

Something Sweet: Sweet Potato Cheesecake

Something Spice: El Yucateco Chile Habanero Green

Song: Perfect Girl by Layma

Ancestor(s): Octavia Butler

Spirit Animal: Owl

Mystery Ingredient: Music

Dear Sis, I Love and See You

Dear Sis,

While cultivating souls, you wear a mask of duplicity
Ever-present yet unnoticed
Pouring yourself empty
because you were born to heal

You've cloaked yourself in invisibility
Present but no presence
Hidden in plain sight
Because often, crowded rooms are lonely

Your love language is acts of service
Giving fluidly
Serving graciously
Remember, while feeding the masses, don't forget to feed yourself
I see us as mirror images, two of a kind
See your name is embellished in the fabric of my legacy
hand-stitched and knitted together
past, present, and future
because your name echoes when mine is called

So, while you cultivate
While you hide
And while you serve
I see you and

I love you

April D Steward
November 1977

About April Steward

April Steward is a force to be reckoned with from every angle. She epitomizes Black Girl Magic in its purest form. In addition to being a fantastic mother, daughter, friend, and sister, she is also an amazing person. With a full-time job, completing a graduate degree, being a mother, and working a computer tech job, she manages to do it all with ease. In addition to having various talents and services to offer, she has an unmatched sense of community. It is her goal to ensure that everyone succeeds, and she consistently strives to extend herself and her abilities in order to help them achieve their goals.

Swift, Kalesha S.

Black Girl Magic Recipe

Something Sweet: Madear's Sweet Potato Pie
Something Spicy: My attitude sometimes
Ancestor(s): Madear
Song: With You by Monica
Spirit Animal: Snake
(*renewal, rebirth, and regeneration; calm and gentle but can be dangerous and won't hesitate to harm someone who hurts me but will remain calm if unbothered*)
Mystery Ingredient: I bend but never break

A Letter to the Younger Me

ear Sis,

No one likes to talk about the uncomfortable things,

so, listen closely - let me tell you some things you have to look forward to:

In school you will be teased because of the fullness of your lips,

but don't worry - one day they'll pay for those same kind of lips.

When you finally meet your father, you're *gonna* wish you never did.

Not long after, you're *gonna* search for the love that your father should've given

you, but instead you'll realize he changed you …

made you not even want the love from a man but only what the man could give you

for that moment.

You're *gonna* look in the mirror, you're gonna cry and ask yourself,
Why? Why am I not enough? Why can't I be loved?

One day, you'll tell yourself, *I can't take care of any more kids.*

Then, alone, you'll just lay there cold, thinking, *Soon it all will be over with.*

You'll learn that it's okay not to be okay.

You will put up with men who will try and tear you down;

you're going to feel low, as if you were under the ground.

But chin up beautiful, readjust your crown.

No, you're not *gonna* have it all figured out,

> but I know without a doubt -
>
> that soon you're *gonna* yell, scream, and shout …
>
> and all that pain will be out.

I love you …

Kalesha S. Swift
November 1985

About Kalesha S. Swift

Kalesha S. Swift is the daughter of Author/Publisher, Iris M. Williams. The 36-year-old beauty is a mom to three beautiful children: Lyric, Jordan, and Landon.

Kalesha graduated from J. A. Fair High School (Little Rock, Arkansas) and earned a Bachelor of Science in Business from the University of Phoenix.

She feels blessed to earn a living doing what she loves, working with children. She also enjoys listening to old-school R&B, writing poetry, and watching Lifetime movies.

Swift, Lyric N.

Black Girl Magic Recipe

Something Sweet: Ice Cream

Something Spicy: Hot Chips

Song: Just Fine by Mary J. Blige

Ancestor(s): My mom

Spirit Animal: Polar Bear

Mystery Ingredient: My relationship with my brother, Landon (Mac)

Black Girl Magic – Beauty and Power

ear Sis,

Black Girl Magic is power and beauty. Black Girl Magic lets me know that I can do anything I put my mind to!

When I was 12, I began to battle depression. At the age of 13, I was admitted to a behavioral health hospital. I was there for two to three weeks. At the age of 14, I attempted suicide. I overdosed on my depression medication and almost killed myself. My younger brother, Landon, found me. When I was released from the hospital, I was readmitted to the behavioral health facility. When I was 15, my life began to change. I became close to God. When I was 16, I was doing well, but I made a mistake and lost my "V card" to a 19-year-old.

I got back on track. At the age of 17, my life was great. I was focused on myself and God. I was happy with my family and was learning new things. My mom helped me realize the Black Girl Magic in me. Now, I know that I can do anything I put my mind to. *"I can do all things through Christ who strengthens me." Philippians 4:13*

I love you ...

Lyric N. Swift
November 2003

About Lyric N. Swift

Lyric "AKA Nevaeh" Swift is the oldest daughter of Kalesha S. Swift and the oldest grandchild of Author/Publisher, Iris M. Williams. The 5"7', 18-year-old beauty is a senior at Southwest High School.

At some point, Lyric plans to attend college and to pursue a profession in nursing. Before that she wants to take a break from school to do hair and work at a childcare facility.

Lyric's favorite color is blue, she loves seafood, music (Mary J. Blige is her favorite), making TikTok videos, hair and makeup, and spending time with her family.

"I'm nice if you nice," she says, spoken like a young woman who has that Black Girl Magic!

Taylor, Kara

Black Girl Magic Recipe

Something Sweet: Sincere compliments from a friend

Something Spicy: Red pepper flakes

Ancestor(s): Ida B. Wells

Song: I Owe You Nothing by Seinabo Sey

Spirit Animal: Lion

Mystery Ingredient: Faith

love grows Here

Black. Woman. Sister.

ear Sis,

Sister? Sister.

So… between you and me… I am not the one to write in this forum. It's not the writing that gets me. It is me who does not belong here. What do I know of Black sisterhood? What experiences can I offer that would be of any use on this topic? From being the only Black family in my Southern Baptist church to being one of very few Black students taking honors courses in school to being the only Black student in my degree field in college; my experiences of Black female friendships are scarce to the point of being nonexistent. My story does not seem to…fit. I guess, in the same way, I have never fit in with Black women. I have spent my entire life on the outside-looking-in on Black community and culture. Growing up, I only spent time with Black folks with whom I shared a common ancestor. And, since I'm being honest, I didn't really feel I belonged, even there. What would be the use of trying to connect with women who have no tie to me?

From my perspective, Black sisterhood is a beautiful dream, one that you try to go back to sleep for a few more minutes to enjoy. It was something longed-for that I could never make exist in my reality, a Christmas movie version of someone else's experiences. My efforts to manifest this dream always required compromise to the point of disintegration on my part. I can be part of "us" if I were willing to sacrifice essential pieces of me. Had I tried joining a sorority or sought Black professional groups, perhaps I could tell a different story. Truthfully, it is likely something is wrong with me that prevents me from feeling this longed-for attachment. As it stands, my long-held belief that Black women just don't like me has been met with very little contrary evidence. I have felt tolerated not celebrated in that circle, acknowledged but never really accepted. And, eventually, I have learned to do without. Some dreams remain elusive, no matter what you speak into existence or what compromises you are prepared to make to obtain them. Not everyone gets to experience the dream.

I suppose that is why I write. Not everyone has the same experience of Blackness, sisterhood, or even womanhood. For those feeling that they come up short, I can relate. For those who feel Black sisterhood from an infinite distance, approaching but never quite reaching, I feel the same, girl, same, I no longer choose to force relationships of any kind. I show up for myself in the fullness of my experience, whether it is shared or not. I have much experience of womanhood and being Black in predominately White spaces that allows me to see others in the same circumstance. I take those opportunities I have both to commiserate and encourage others as the moments arise and to be the sister I wish I had in similar situations. While I can't say I have a close group of sisters, I have given myself permission to validate my own experience. A part of me will always crave a sense of belonging in that circle. I could never deny these two parts of myself that vastly shaped and continue to influence how I move in this world, but I no longer adjust myself to try to fit. I have discovered that rejection of others doesn't sting when you have accepted yourself. Black. Woman. Sister. That I am. I am all of that.

 I love you …

Kara Taylor
August 1986

About Kara Taylor

Kara Taylor is a pediatric speech-language pathologist. She is delighted by terrible jokes, Yes Days, and is wholly committed to the Oxford comma.

Tims, Kassidi

Black Girl Magic Recipe

Something Sweet: Kit Kats

Something Spicy: Hot Cheetos

Ancestor(s): Nanny (*Earleane Buchanan*)

Song: Single Ladies by Beyonce

Spirit Animal: Cheeta

Mystery Ingredient: Purple Passion Flowers

Dear Kennedi

ear Sis,

Kennedi (my sister) –

Thank you for all you've done.

You're my everything. You're my number one.

You have been with me along the way,

and you are sometimes the only thing that makes me happy,

but know that I'm ok.

We've been through a lot of things.

I hope people see that I love you & you love me.

I look up to you. Can you tell?

I hope that you're really well.

When we get older, I must say I will think about you every day.

I love you in every way.

Dear Kennedi, thank you for all you've done.

You're my everything. You're my number one. ♥

I love you …

Kassadi Tims
February 2010

About Kassadi Tims

Kassadi Tims is a charismatic twelve-year-old from Little Rock, Arkansas. She is the daughter of Mario and Neitasha Tims. She is a 7th grader at Forest Heights Stem Academy. Kassadi loves all things science, cheer, and acting. When she grows up, she wants to be a medical engineer and to invent the devices that cure cancer. Her motto in life is "Sometimes you just have to wing it."

Trichel, Kenzi

Black Girl Magic Recipe

Something Sweet: My voice

Something Spicy: My figure

Song: Masterpiece (Mona Lisa) by Jazmine Sullivan

Ancestor(s): Magical

Spirit Animal: Cat

Mystery Ingredient: Education

Be love.
Be light.

Being A Woman

ear Sis,

Growing up, my momma instilled three things in all her children: get your education, get a stable job, get married, and have kids. That was the assignment, and I understood it well. I graduated from Philander Smith College in 2010. I graduated from the University of Arkansas at Little Rock in 2014 with a Masters in Social Work. I currently work at Arkansas Children's Hospital as a social worker on the cardiovascular intensive care unit. I have spoken about treating Black women who carry the superwoman cape. I've even spoken on the complicated relationship between Black men and their mental health, both of which were done at Yale University (slight brag). On paper, ya girl is looking good.

While achieving those things was not an easy feat during that time, they came natural to me. I knew the steps I needed to take to achieve those things. I knew failure was an option but not for me. I knew what I wanted to do, and I had an amazing support system that carried me. So naturally, I thought getting married and having kids would essentially be the same. I was so wrong. I can spend days talking about the complexities of dating while being a therapist and having issues with being vulnerable. However, that is not the point of this story.

Like most Black households, it was normal to be asked, "When are you going to have kids?" It became very common as my nephew grew older. My sister is naturally a nurturer and has been responsible for "raising" several babies. She was instrumental in my raising, so she couldn't wait to get her hands on one of my babies. Honestly, there was a part of me that could not wait. My momma is probably the best granny on the planet, and she was just excited about the possibility. From her perspective, she wanted to be able to be as involved in my kids' life as she was in my nephew's. We had all given up hope that my brother would have kids of his own. He did us one better though and brought three boys and a little girl into our lives.

There wasn't much talk about forming healthy relationships and later having the baby. I remember often letting them know that I would have a baby when I met my husband. When I think back on it now, I cannot help but laugh because never in a million years did I think that finding a husband would be the least of my worries in the future. During this time, I found myself in fake love and situationships disguised as relationships. Yet, my brain was focused on this idea of family completion that included a healthy relationship and babies with no experience in either nor a guide as to what it looked like and how to get there.

Towards the end of 2010, I noticed that something was going on with my menstrual cycle. I would have cramps that had me lying on the floor at work unable to move let alone do my job. They were super heavy and became more frequent; it wasn't normal. I was diagnosed with an extreme case of endometriosis, which is when tissue that lines the uterus grows outside of the uterus. In my case, it was doing major damage to my ovaries. So, in January 2011, I had my first procedure to give me the best chance at having babies in the future. Notice, I didn't say a better quality of life. I know it played a role in it, but I was focused on this baby.

Back then, the information I received was that endometriosis is basically cured by having a baby. Cool, cool, cool, my thought was *So, I could have avoided this by having a baby out of wedlock* (insert eye roll)? This procedure was done laparoscopically and on an outpatient basis. The follow-up treatment was a monthly Lupron injection that put me in a medically induced menopausal state for six months. Oh, and my doctor at the time also informed me that ideally, I would need to have a baby in the next three years, or it would come back. I guess the doctor didn't know that I needed a husband to make that happen, not to mention, more added pressure to have a baby.

I'll skip through the next few years of me searching for my husband so I can have this baby. I now know that I spent so much of the time in situationships based off of ONE husband potential quality. Ya girl was out here ignoring red flags, red lights, sirens, and all of it because I was so focused on a single quality.

Fast forward to 2017, I remember the day so clearly because it was so traumatic for me. Even sitting here thinking about it brings me anxiety and brings tears to my eyes. I went to work like normal, but I noticed that I was short of breath. I just thought it was my asthma because it had moments like that. Slowly, I went about my day, walking back and forth to the school to pull my clients for their individual and family therapy sessions. I was excited because, after work, I was going to my friend Kim's house to play Bingo and make Chex Mix. I truly was minding my business, and that evening, out of nowhere, my cycle started. I thought it was weird because it was not time, and it was heavier than normal.

I went on about my business but consciously because I was no longer feeling well. I left Hot Springs and made it home around 9 or 10. Then, all hell broke loose. I was bleeding through everything with huge clots. I went to the emergency room, and I sat there for hours, bleeding and waiting for them to call me back in hopes of finding some answers. They called me back after three or four hours for what felt like a 15-minute assessment by a resident of some sort. He looked down there, did some cleaning out, and gave me some bullshit reason. He made it clear that he was not sure because he could not get a clear visual of my uterus or cervix because there was so much blood. He gave me a prescription for birth control, told me to schedule with my OB, and sent me home.

I get home, still bleeding through everything and lie down. I didn't go to sleep. Eventually, I went to my bathroom to set up shop for the night because I was still bleeding through everything. At this point, I was scared. I called my mom feeling weak with ringing in my ears. She told me to call an ambulance. She called my aunt and was on her way. My mom lived in Eudora which was two and a half hours away. The fire department showed up first, and let me tell you, there is nothing more embarrassing than two to three men seeing you in no underwear surrounded by blood. Once the ambulance arrived, I explained what was going on, and they asked if I wanted to go back to the hospital from which I just came. "Hell no!" I later found out that I was moments from fainting due to blood loss.

I was almost immediately admitted to the second hospital due to a low blood count. It's important to note that I was only home for two hours before calling the ambulance. While waiting for a bed to be ready for me, I let my supervisor know what was going on and simultaneously making plans to return to work in a day or two. They determined that I needed a blood transfusion. During this hospitalization, they found Phyliss. Phyliss is the name I gave my three to four pound fibroid. I figured that if the heifa was going to take up residence, she needed a name and Phyliss fit. Anyway, Phyliss was big…she had me walking around looking six months pregnant. I thought it was just weight gain because I love snacks. Most of the doctors who came into my room during that hospitalization spoke with me about a hysterectomy. I'm not exaggerating; no one offered me another option.

At the time, that was not an option for me. I was only 28 years old with no husband and no kids. Didn't I deserve a chance to figure out if I wanted children or not? Shouldn't that be my choice? How would I find a husband while not being able to give him children? These were the questions and concerns with which I left the hospital.

At my follow-up appointment, I met my doctor/surgeon. When explaining my story to her, she was the first doctor that said, "We can remove it, if you would like." She gave me a choice. She gave me hope. She listened to me. I did another round of Lupron shots in hopes of slowing the growth of Phyliss and shrinking the heifa. During the time leading up to the surgery, I threw myself into work. I prepared to be away for four to six weeks and tried to figure out how I was going to continue to get paid while away because I did not earn a lot of PTO. I was on call for the entire month of September because I earned PTO when I was on call. In addition to this, I arranged with my supervisor to continue to do my treatment plans and participate with team members to save PTO.

I'm happy to say that the procedure was a success. I kept my uterus, cervix, and ovaries; I was still a woman with choices. I was given more time to figure out if I wanted children. My mom was so supportive of me during this time. My two best friends, at the time, took such good care of me and my cat, Bash. I stayed with them while I recovered because I couldn't drive and could not do a lot of things on my own those first few weeks. With this second chance, it was time to get serious about finding a husband. At this point, my mind shifted to finding a husband because who wants a woman that does not have a uterus (insert cycle of situationships)?

It's weird because it was during this season that I really threw myself into projects outside of my full-time job. I started working in private practice part time, I was working on presentations with my partner in crime, and I was busy. For the next four years, that's what I did. I started therapy in 2018 following the traumatic loss of a mentor. I continued to have these conversations with family and friends about having children. Honestly, it depended on who I was talking to. There were cycles in which I knew I wanted kids. In fact, in 2019, I was talking to my friends and family about using a sperm donor. I started doing research and was determined. I don't think I had given up on the husband piece, but I was now okay with not being married before having children. I had the support of my family; my sister even offered to let the baby stay with her. I can honestly say I was all over the place when it came to this. I also was living my best life traveling and speaking. I really miss that time. Things were stressful, but I was maneuvering and dodging while sitting with it all.

Towards the end of March, a familiar pain and lethargy snuck up on me, but it was different. Based on my history, I knew I needed to make an appointment with my OB/GYN. I had not been to the doctor since 2019 because of the pandemic. I wasn't able to get in to see my doctor, but I was able to see the APRN. I went through my normal spill and history except, this time, I requested all the tests be run including a blood draw to make sure my levels were good. She ordered an ultrasound and put me on fairly strong pain medication. The ultrasound did not show anything significant…a few fibroids but nothing that should have accounted for the pain exhaustion I felt.

I'm grateful that she listened to me and took my pain seriously. She even checked on me the following day which was a new experience for me. Due to the amount of pain I was in, she sent me to UAMS for a CT scan and pain management. I let my supervisor know because I would be running late for work, but I was still planning to come in. I had been working in pain for weeks, so that was not going to stop me. The CT scan showed a mass, and they were concerned it was cancer. By this point, my aunt was with me, my momma was on her way, and I was freaking out. Cancer? How? My dad had just been diagnosed two weeks prior; my step mom had died a week prior. Who had time and the emotional capacity for Cancer? Thank God it wasn't me. I did have a tumor, but it was not cancerous. The tumor did mean that I would need a complete hysterectomy. I would have my cervix, uterus, and fallopian tubes removed. If I were lucky, I would get to keep my ovaries and not have to undergo hormone therapy.

My surgical team was led by Dr. Savage, a gynecologist oncologist with amazing reviews. I briefly met him before discharging from the hospital because I wasn't leaving without speaking with him and hearing from his mouth what the plan would be. When I followed up with him in the clinic, he came in with my scans and loads of information. While reviewing everything with me, I felt numb and scared. I don't remember much from the conversation, but I remember him telling me, "There isn't anything worth saving." My heart dropped and a flood of tears and thoughts came rushing at me. My ovaries were covered in endometriosis, and there were multiple cysts in one of them. He told me that he might be able to leave one, but he made me no promises. He told me that if he left it, I would need to be prepared for another surgery in the future to have it removed. I told him I needed to think about it, but when I left, I knew that this would be my last surgery regarding my uterus.

I was sent home on bedrest with an around the clock pain medication regimen until my surgery date. When I tell you that my tribe showed up for me, they showed up! They sat with me in silence. If I needed to process something out loud, they gave me space to do that without feedback. They fed me, cleaned for me, and most importantly, they prayed for me and with me. Man did they pray for me! I know for a fact that I made it through based on the prayers of others because there were days when I felt I could not pray for myself. When my momma was not with my stepdad being his fulltime caregiver, she was with me being mine. When she wasn't available, my aunt showed up. I am forever grateful for my tribe.

The day of my surgery, my mom and I showed up bright and early. They told my mom it would be three hours, and I believe it was only two. When I woke up, I was in so much pain. Typically, they don't move you until your pain is under control. They struggled with this, and that goal was not accomplished. I believe that it was largely in part to the fact that I had been on a strong pain medication regimen before surgery. I made it to my room right at their shift change. I remember requesting for my night bedside nurse to come to my room for introductions. That never happened. In addition to that, I was still in pain. We called for the nurse several times, and no one came. When the tech came to do my vitals, we made the same request. It was so long, and my pain was so bad that my mom went into the hallway several times making the same request.

By the time my nurse came in, she had an attitude with me. As I was telling her about my pain, she sputtered out the times I had pain medication. I was starting to feel that she did not take my pain seriously and that I was pain med seeking. I was pissed, and I was crying. I requested to speak with the team lead and explained my concerns to her. She contacted the doctor because she felt my pain needed to be re-evaluated. I think it was heart breaking because I was speaking with two Black women. During this time, I was so upset. I was apologizing for being upset because I was not problematic. I worked at a hospital, so I knew how it was. The doctor came in to evaluate and make some changes so I could be more comfortable. It was during this time that she asked if my blood had been drawn. Apparently, I had lost a significant amount of blood during surgery, and they were concerned that I would need more blood in addition to what I received in the OR. This request had been put in HOURS prior. I was pissed. I requested not to see that nurse again.

I'm grateful that the rest of my experience went without difficulties. I was grateful for that because I knew all of my energy would need to be preserved for the time when I was ready to start grieving this loss. I'm not there, but telling this story is the foundation to my healing. Brene Brown stated, "If you put shame in a Petri dish, it needs three things to grow exponentially: secrecy, silence, and judgment. If you put the same amount of shame in a Petri dish and douse it with empathy, it can't survive." My prayer is that by sharing my story I start to walk with empathy and grace for myself. I have fertilized my fertility struggle with secrecy, silence, and judgment for so long that the shame in myself has overgrown. It's time that I start to trim it back.

To my sisters who are reading this story, my prayer is that as you maneuver through the journey of what it means to be a woman, that you don't mistake it as being the same as childbearing. With or without children, you are a woman. I pray that should you decide that you want to have kids, the decision is for yourself and not because society says this is something you should want or need. Make the decision for yourself, not for your family, partner, friends, or anyone else. To my sisters who are on a journey similar to mine, advocate for your body. There is not a person in this entire world who knows your body better than you do. If your medical providers will not listen to you, make them. If they cannot provide you with the care that you need and deserve, fire them and find someone else. My sister, your body is precious and deserves care and treatment as such.

I love you …

Kenzi Trichel
July 1988

About Kenzi Trichel

From a fairly young age, Mackenzi knew that she wanted to help people, more specifically, that she wanted to be a therapist. So, that is exactly what she became. Over the years of being a therapist, she has found her voice not only as a woman but as a Black woman. She has passionately worked to bring awareness to what it means to be a Black woman and wear a superwoman cape. She has used her voice to speak on this subject in spaces such as the National Association of Social Work Conference and Yale University. She has taught Diversity and Oppression to master level social workers. Over the last year, she has poured into the space of perinatal mental health. That journey has led to the opening of Holding Space Counseling, a therapy practice catering to women through their journey of becoming a mother, motherhood, and grief. She holds a special love for working with Black women as she recognizes the need for Black women to find safety in other Black women. She thrives on being a safe space for others.

WADE, VONETTA

Black Girl Magic Recipe

Something Sweet: Warm fudge brownies

Something Spicy: Nachos w/hot peppers

Ancestor(s): Sula Mae Longs

Song: Black Butterfly by Deniece Williams

Spiritual Animal: Deer

Mystery Ingredient: Authenticity

Love, Support, and Forgiveness

ear Sis,

You are special and unique. Embrace it. You were made perfectly for the purpose you were designed to serve. Your reason for being and your journey are different from mine. You cannot be me, and I cannot be you. There is no need to compare or compete. Instead, let us help each other accomplish our purpose. Imagine how much better off we all would be if we truly became the people we were created to be.

When I think of sisterhood, the words that come to my mind are ***love***, ***support***, and ***forgiveness***. Through these poems, I am sharing what I have learned and know to be true. This is what I want generations of Blacks girls to know.

Love

Love is something we all desire.

It creates a feeling of wholeness and sets our hearts on fire.

When we experience love, we feel like there is nothing we cannot do.

Sis, always remember that the greatest love you'll ever experience is the love you have for you.

So many of us take the endless journey of looking for love elsewhere and in the wrong places.

It could leave us lost, hurt, and abandoned in some cases.

"It is ok to be alone, and you do not need to be with anyone," are wise words often spoken.

It is better to be by yourself than to be in a bad relationship trying to fix someone who is broken.

We must dig deep inside to understand what we want and who we really are.

Remember that support from your sisters is not very far.

Reach out because we will always be there.

We will give you a shoulder to cry on because we care.

It is important to keep your sisters near even when your relationship is going great.

Find a balance between nourishing your sisterhood and romance with your mate.

Sis, never lose yourself, and if you choose wisely, you will not have to.

Sisterhood and love for self are important because both will help you find your way back to you.

Support

We all need support, and we expect our sisters to be there as much as possible.

I have learned that people have limitations, and when they are not, it is not always personal.

Your sisters could be mentally unavailable or experiencing undisclosed pain.

Keep this in mind, sis and avoid feelings of anger or disdain.

People cannot give what they do not have, so offer them some grace.

Trust God as He has a way of sending what and who you need at the right time and place.

Understand that your support may change and be open to embracing new sisterhood.

There are new relationships to build and new things to learn, and this is all working for your good.

If you have a sister who is still focused on holding you up even when she is down,

hold on to her for dear life. She is to be cherished and given her sisterhood crown.

Go sis go, and even though everyone cannot go along with you as you travel your road to success,

please know dear sis, that we are all wishing you the best.

Forgiveness

When your sister offends or hurts you,

having a crucial conversation is the most uncomfortable thing to do.

It is easier to get upset and shut down in silence,

But this never gives her the opportunity to understand her offence.

The relationship changes and only one person knows the reason why.

Your sis deserves an opportunity to correct her wrongs or at least try.

We cannot expect people to guess how we feel.

Being open and honest is not easy, but it is important if the friendship is real.

Once you explain what your sis did to make you feel some type of way,

you will know how the relationship moves forward based on what she has to say.

If she is not willing to acknowledge or respect your point of view, then distance may be fine.

We all fall short, but we also must protect ourselves and our peace of mind.

But if she is genuine and the charge is forgivable, please do so and handle her with grace.

Good friends are rare, so consider yourself blessed and move forward at your own pace.

I love you …

Vonetta Wade
March 1973

About Vonetta Wade

Vonetta Wade is a modern-day renaissance woman. She overcame the challenges of being a teen mom and developed the audacity to succeed and inspire others. She is an author and co-author, certified life coach focused on parent-child relationships, mindfulness, and life purpose, has a 501(c)(3) nonprofit geared towards mentoring youth to a brighter future and supporting parents, and she is an authentic and practical leader at a fortune 100 company empowering her organization to adapt an agile mindset. Understanding the significance of words, Vonetta intentionally speaks life and positivity to all in her space. Her most significant and proudest achievement is having both her children graduate from college. People are her passion, and changing lives is her purpose. Vonetta recently received an Honorary Doctorate Degree from the Trinity International University of Ambassadors (TIUA), School of Business in June 2022.

WHITE, JAI

Black Girl Magic Recipe

Something Sweet: Slushy

Something Spicy: Hot Cheetos

Ancestor(s): Dorothy Brown (*Great Grandma*)

Song: Time Machine by Muni Long

Spirit Animal: Rabbit

Mystery Ingredient: Rest and Sleep

Sisters and Loving

Dear Sis,

In my life, sisterhood is about coming together as sisters and loving one another. I have a sis that is a best friend, cousin, and a leader. We might not have the same mother or father, but I still count her as my sis. I might not show it, and she might not know it. I notice that she gets good grades in school, and I look up to her. She is a best friend, cousin, and sister.

I love you …

Jai White
July 2011

About Jai White

Jai is the only child of Katina White. She is a lover of learning and life. At school, Jai is a member of the National Beta Club, an organization for 4th through 12th grade students. Its purpose is "to promote the ideals of academic achievement, character, leadership, and service among elementary and secondary school students." She is on the Robotics Team, and she really likes math. She loves music and dancing. Her favorite song is Time Machine by Money Long. Artists she enjoys are Chika, Jay Z, and Muni Long. Recently, Jai added to her growing list of interests and activities by joining an Arkansas AAU Track Team. This budding athlete enjoys the events of shot put, discus, and javelin. When not achieving scholastically or competing in sports, Jai enjoys hanging out with family, going to church, and conducting all kinds of science experiments.

She is also the owner and CEO of Jai's Lip Gloss, a cosmetic company with products created by the scientist and entrepreneur herself.

Williams, Iris M.

Black Girl Magic Recipe

Something Sweet: Lemon Meringue Pie

Something Spicy: Tajin

Ancestor(s): Maya Angelou

Song: Born for This by Bebe Winans & Stephanie Mills

Spirit Animal: Black Butterfly

Mystery Ingredient: Laughter

Giving

ear Sis,

For more than 30-years of my life, I carried the weight of shame and blame due to childhood molestation, parental abandonment, multiple marriages, and the heartbreak of placing a child for adoption at the age of 17. In 2013, I left a lucrative career, my children, and moved more than a thousand miles away from family and friends to pursue what I believed to be a forever love, only to realize it was not to be. I returned to Arkansas broken – emotionally, mentally, and financially.

I felt rejected.

I tried to be a nun and was rejected because I was too old.

I tried suicide, and even death rejected me.

Finally, I tried God, and thankfully, I was accepted!

Giving In

For me, Black Girl Magic is about finding and living a life of purpose. Life looks good and feels good when you are purpose-filled, and people respond to you differently. You are focused and passionate. You get more done, and your successes are more than your losses because more of your time is spent in the same arena. You aren't wasting time on things that do not matter. In this way, even when you fail, you learn – making your next attempt better than the last.

I've found that when you operate in your purpose, much of what you do seems to come naturally. Consequently, you're less stressed and happier. You glow. In other words, you have that "Black Girl Magic!"

Before I got the glow, I felt something was missing. By society's standards, I had arrived, but inside, I knew I had not. Instead, I was miserable, and people around me treated me the way I felt. Unfortunately for me, it took the death of a loved one for me to realize that I was wasting precious time. I'd spent many years hiding behind fear. Finally, my brother's early and untimely death awakened me to the fact that death was not reserved for the elderly. I decided I wanted to live and not just exist. And that's how my successful journey to living a Black Girl Magic life began!

Giving Back

I exited bad marriage number three, moved to North Carolina, wrote my first book, and founded a publishing company. The publishing company's purpose was supposed to be about me finally finding a way to write my story, but before that could happen, I would help more than 100 people tell their stories.

Ironically, each story I published helped heal pieces of my broken heart. I published stories about broken marriages, molestation, and much more. I published children's books, memoirs, devotionals, and even erotica! Of course, I was hesitant to publish those types of stories, but I found that it wasn't about the story in those cases – it was about the author and me. Through my life experiences and these authors' stories, I learned to accept others. It really is true. Hurt people, hurt people. Now, instead of judging them, I want to love the hurt away. In essence, each story touched me, and each author impacted my life. I matured in ways that I never dreamed possible.

I found that skills I had long since possessed were now serving me. For instance, as a child, I used to want to be a teacher and a nurse. And now, as a publisher, I was teaching authors how to write and tell their stories. And by listening to them, I was helping to heal their emotional wounds!

Black Girl Magic sets you apart from others. What sets me apart from other publishers is that I can see beyond what is on the paper. Instinctively, I know the order of things, and I can "fill in the gaps" and determine what is missing.

Giving Up

For six years, I worked outside of the corporate world. As a single Black female, things were hard. There were many days I wasn't sure if what I was doing was the right thing, but when I contemplated giving up, the journey back seemed just as far as going forward, so I pushed ahead. I know what it is like to have .76 cents and no credit cards, upcoming payday, savings, or anyone to turn to for help. I know what it is like to go to bed with hunger pains and wake up with those same pains.

One Sunday as I sat in church, an advertisement for an administrative assistant captured my attention. After the service, I went to my car and called the number. I scheduled an interview the next day and was hired on the spot. The job started right away. Instead of my cubicle being in the main office with the other administrative personnel, I was placed in the food pantry building. Every day, I sat surrounded by rooms filled with food, with a growling stomach and a swelling pride.

One afternoon, Teresa, the lady who administered the program, came to my desk and handed me a form.

"Fill this out," she said, "and give it back to me. Then, every month you can take a box home. And before you leave today, grab a box and get whatever you want from the walk-in freezer."

I couldn't say anything. By this time, I was too hungry to protest. So instead, with tears in my eyes, I nodded my head in thanks.

Later, I handed her the form and took a box into the freezer. To my delight, it was filled with fresh items from Sam's. Most of the items were things I regularly purchased. Until then, I thought the food pantry donated old, expired food. I was given so much food. I even had enough to share with my daughter and her family!

I realized that my Black Girl Magic was evident even when I didn't operate in my purpose. My light was a beacon so that help could find me even when I didn't have the sense to ask for it!

Did things get better right away? No. Has every day after been easy? Absolutely not. But easy was not the promise. The promise was that I wouldn't have to go at it alone. And I haven't. My advice to anyone is this: skip the scenic route to purpose. It may seem like fun, but trust me, it isn't. I recently marveled that I have been single now for more than seven years. Just as I was about to get depressed about that, I realized that I've also not had my heart broken more than seven years.

I recently returned to the corporate world. God has not only restored me but has actually elevated me past where I was when I left in 2013. I'm so thankful. I want anyone who encounters me or reads my story to know that it is never too late, that you can do it, and that whatever your purpose (or Black Girl Magic) – you matter. No one can take it away, and no one can do it the way you can do it. You glow, girl!

My story, "An Abundant Life," is available in paperback, hardback, ebook and audiobook. However, as we approach a new year, I look forward to coming from behind the publisher's desk, sitting behind the mic, and standing behind the podium to share my story – live and in person. I no longer seek to be hidden, but I want to be seen and heard. I have a story to tell – a Black Magic Girl story, and it's essential.

How do I know that?

Here's how:

> *"And they overcome him by the blood of the lamb and the word of their testimony;"*
> Revelation 12:11

I love you …

Iris M. Williams
July 1969

About Iris M. Williams

Iris M. Williams is an author, writer, and publisher. She works for a local insurance company as a Regulatory Compliance Analyst and owns Butterfly Typeface Publishing in Little Rock, Arkansas. The mother of two and Nana of five enjoys spending time with family and friends, crafting stories, solving puzzles, traveling, and listening to music.

The multi-published author can be contacted via authorirismwilliams@gmail.com, butterflytypeface.imw@gmail.com, or you may visit her websites at www.irismwilliams.com and www.butterflytypeface.com.

WILLIAMS, KENDRA

Black Girl Magic Recipe

Something Sweet: Sweet Potato Crème Brulee

Something Spicey: Honey sweetened Peri-Peri with a sprinkle of smoked paprika

Ancestor(s): All the ones who breathed for me until I arrived

Song:

Spirit Animal: Coral

Mystery Ingredient: The pot liquor in any southern dish. (*I add substance.*)

My Iridium Sister

Dear Sis,

If I am being honest, I faintly remember being loved

Being wrapped in spirit and plans…

To know heart, apart from longing

An easy knowing

A considerate gesture just because

A love I have never seen outside of the television screen

And I long for its' deepening

Has probably come and gone without my emotional presence -

Because it is DANGEROUS being caught A Caring Black Woman

When reciprocity has no sense of treasure

No back to be had unless there is ass up

No truths accepted unless vested by the shortcomings coming towards us

But I am here

Completely by choice

However, there is necessity

Here to hold your hand

I know how tightly fingers and hands press together when been bent backwards before

Here to listen attentively

Too many years of being ignored
Too many detours and closed doors
But I choose you

To be here for you in a different way
To offer the escape this world refuses to loosen its grip upon, but trust

You
Are
Loved

The family tree is rooted *in* you
It should not be carried *by* you
Exhausted from the lack of care for you
I am you
And I dare to support you fiercely

I remind me

Cry with you and hear your woes without the burden of insults thrown
Not contingent on who you were nor decisions you have made
But who you are in your safe space

The place where you are both happiest and most afraid
Where outsiders fade
And there is just You
OR
Cocooned inside of yourself

Where thoughts march from one insult to the next

Vexed and fatigued

Stuck between being enslaved and being free

From extreme zero to fast speed

You Are Loved

The scenery changes when eyes adjust

There is trust, present and ready to embrace you

Every bit of you

The least of you

The exposed parts of you

Your truth

The truth

No woman left down or behind

tersely

We climb -

out of valleys

Into careers we choose

Spiritual walks *in our own* shoes

into destinies we have embedded in our souls

We speak life wherever we land our soles

We sing one another's praises in the faces of all those who disbelieved

We be known as self-fulls

The distance between famine and plenty

royals in everyday existence

Here and strong

Your being matters

YOU matter

And just in case you cannot hear through the clatter

YOU
    ARE
        LOVE

Sincerely yours

Like Nature

I love you …

Kendra Williams

October 1976

About Kendra Williams

My government name is Kendra Williams. I struggled in writing this bio. I decided to tell WHAT I love in an effort to tell WHO I am. I have the most existentially dopest baby ever - my pre-teen queen, Sophie. My daughter is my favorite human on the planet. I, in part, live to see how God will be a blessing through and because of my baby. No bones, nor skin, nor breath, nor theories nor love without my God. SHE is very much the only reason I am.

I am a writer whose words seek to heal.

I am a poet whose words take residence in people's thoughts.

I am a singer whose voice lives in the walls of every place I have ever loved.

I am a chef who is professionally trained from-my-kitchen.

I am learning to love myself more compassionately; to purr instead of roar; to make adventure my new normal.

Mental soundness, being physically healthy, spiritually higher and living in peace are my life's goals. My profession includes helping to form young minds and creating opportunity in a world that seems to try to do the opposite.

I will write a book.

I will be a mentor.

I will travel great distances.

And I will make positive memories for anyone I meet - if they choose.

I will love my entire self, more every day.

Wilson, Rayme

Black Magic Recipe

Something Sweet: Creole white chocolate bread pudding

Something Spicy: The seasoning at a crawfish boil

Ancestor(s): Blanche Perria

Song: Heal the World by Michael Jackson

Spirit Animal: Mermaid

Mystery Ingredient: Gratitude

Made with love

Beautiful You Are

ear Sis,

In you is every hue.

Divine Cosmic attributes.

Sun kissed skin.

Beauty overflowing melanin. Stone strength from within.

Remember to always hold up your chin.

There would be no world without a little Black girl.

I love you …

Rayme C. Wilson
May 1986

About Rayme C. Wilson

Rayme C. Wilson is a New Orleans native turned Arkansan who is committed to being a positive role model for her community. In addition to her love of learning and teaching, she has a passion for people. Over the course of her career, she has spent 90% in education. Whether she is teaching her sons to cook or delivering a motivational speech, Rayme's focus is to help people. Her intent is to lead with love. Rayme's witty personality and smile can brighten up any day. She can find some "sunshine" on a rainy day because of her optimistic personality. She helps people of all backgrounds through her "Leading in Love" life coaching business, "RayOfSunshine LLC." Rayme's formula is "Leading with love is like mathematics, it's universal," and she firmly thinks she can bring sunshine into anyone's life who comes to her.

WILSON, TUDI

Black Girl Magic Recipe

Something Sweet: My love language

Something Spicy: My sarcasm

Song: Fuckin Perfect by Pink

Ancestor(s): Grace Jones

Spirit Animal: Hummingbird

Mystery Ingredient: Pixie dust in my pinky finger

What I Wish My Mom Had Told Me

ear Sis,

I'm unsure of when I got here, stuck between. Frankly, I don't and give a fuck.
No one gets mad at the dumpster for holding trash or filling the garbage truck.

Serving purpose with promised intent
No room on the bench where the fat kids sit

Outcasted by idiots with mediocre intellect,
common sense gives no scholarships

I sat behind gyrating hips, sex moans,
and no home phones

Where the hoods and fast asses collect
reflect on faux experience trying to seem grown,

And I wonder if I ever wanted to fit in.
These motherfuckers couldn't be my friends
cause I was NOT impressed.

However, I became stressed as a target of ridicule

Wondering why I couldn't or didn't look like all the bitches I loathed,
why I felt uncomfortable in my clothes.

Was it the fabric or shape that filled the pockets
or the boobs that filled the bralettes?

I don't know, and I wondered was I ugly or intimidating because I needed a friend maybe two 6th grade D cups made me a magnet for bad ass maggots seeking titles in elementary school.

Never cool, just friendly, covered but not trendy
because being me became a competition with the ugly friends that sat on the bench

Followed by the stench of insecurity, we became the group of friends that didn't fit, and we became everything our bullies would aspire to be….

And see this is what I wish my mom had told me:

- Even ugly and insecure motherfuckers have opinions, and what they think of you is none of your business.
- Do what you love, and you will never work a day in your life.
- Always trust your gut; it won't steer you wrong.
- Find a few songs for tough times.
- Know/understand a few scriptures to keep your spirit happy.
- Value yourself without compromise.
- Embrace your body and love everything about you, love yourself, you deserve it!
- Everyone has a motive, good or bad.
- Don't let them/it break you; you are resilient!
- Lose interest, not sleep.
- Beat the ass of the bully.
- You are not always right.
- Study hard, stupid is a choice.
- You don't have to do it all by yourself; life isn't a solo act.
- The three hardest things to say are: I need help, I was wrong, and I'm sorry.
- Don't let your fears consume and prohibit you from what you want.
- Make your own mistakes.
- The real world doesn't govern under the laws of this house.
- Be the peacock amongst the pigeons.
- Forgive yourself and them but keep the lesson.

- Correct them EVERY SINGLE TIME they come for you.
- Show them who you are unapologetically.
- Everyone has a something (flaw).
- You owe no explanations or apologies for your honesty.
- No is sufficient without further comment.
- Learn conflict resolution.
- Be kind to yourself and embrace everything you don't understand … we are under construction.
- Know when to walk away.
- Don't play small; you are enough because God's grace is sufficient.
- There is enough room in the sky for everyone to fly…support the cause!
- If you don't want to help them, you don't have to hurt them either.
- Teach EVERYONE how to treat you.
- You don't have to be liked, be respected.
- Pick quarter friends to equal a dollar… no dealings in small change.
- You are going to get hurt and disappointed. You will heal; it takes time.
- Mean people have an insecurity issue.
- Pick your battles… some shit ain't worth it!
- Be intentional, confident, and comfortable.
- Be grateful. Why would God bless you with more just to be more ungrateful?
- Your power lies in your tongue; you become what you speak, good or bad.
- It's OK to seek therapy.
- Silence to show anger or disdain isn't effective adulting. Let 'em have it!
- You don't have to negotiate your worth, happiness, and integrity.
- Leave your house dressed like it matters because it does-ALWAYS!
- It's ok to be selfish sometimes.
- Trust God's heart when you can't trace His hand (Have faith no matter what).
- Know how to receive love and compliments from a man.
- You don't always have to be strong.

- Just because you're struggling doesn't mean you are failing.
- Time is irreplaceable… spend it wisely.
- Stand up for what you love and believe in; protect your peace at all costs.
- It's OK to say "Fuck" it, this/that, or you.

Hocus Pocus.

I love you …

Tudi Wilson
July 1982

About Tudi Wilson

I was born Shamarra Garmon, but I am better known as Tudi Wilson. I am a woman with a big heart and multiple talents leaving footprints on the world one step at time. I am a big sister, daughter, aunt, cousin, friend, and asshole sometimes. Nonetheless, I love who I am and am becoming on this journey. I have been fighting for my eyesight since 2017 which has taught me patience, compassion. And the true meaning of a support system. I've learned to be grateful for all things, big and small. My favorite quote is: "When I stand before God at the end of my life, I would hope that I have not a single bit of talent left. Therefore, I could say I used everything you gave me." – Erma Boebeck

I spend my days working toward this goal and making this quote my reality.

Writes, Drekkia

Black Girl Magic Recipe

Something Sweet: Honey buns

Something Spicy: Jalapeños on movie nachos

Ancestor(s): Maya Angelou

Song: What is it? by Webbie

Spirit Animal: Mockingbird

Mystery Ingredient: Crazy Faith

When Is It Valid?

Dear Sis,

When is a woman's "No" valid?
Is it when she fights, screams, or cries?
Does not a gentle "No" mean no?
When I'm aiming my semi-automatic pistol
to your face,
will you then believe me that I was not interested in having sex?
You can't peer pressure this pussy
can't take my belongings
and walk away with a smile.
I will make sure you feel me
with every fiber in my being.
When is a woman's "No" valid?
Is it because we were engaged
in a passionate kiss
that you thought it meant
you had permission to try me,
to attempt to push me past my comfort zone
when I had already clearly said "No"?
You may have thought I said no

in attempt to pretend like

"I don't usually do this,"

"I'm not a hoe," or "I don't do one-night stands."

You may have thought

I was trying to play coy, quaint, and cute.

But I assure you… you're confused

Because if I wanted to fuck, that's exactly what I'd do.

Is it because I did not yell or curse you out

the first time I declined your gentle advances that you did not take me seriously?

Must a woman cut your tongue

and slice your ego

for you to understand that no means NO.

Did you think if you tried to touch my pussy over and over again that I would give in?

Were you hoping you could softly coerce me into submission?

When is a woman's "No" valid?

Is it ever?

For centuries women have been broken under bedsheets of shame and secrecy

harboring the burden of another man's demons

dying inside,

while unintentionally giving him more power and confidence to create more victims like you.

You know the kind that gets their voice taken away,

won't stand up,

and is constantly buried in pain

The kind that's full of self-blame,

unreasonable shame,

one that's left to never trust again,

can't open up

because they've been closed off so long

they think hiding in their trauma is safer than speaking up and living with the aftermath

that may come with telling the truth.

Will a woman's "No" ever be valid?

I love you ...

Drekkia Writes
October 1993

About Drekkia Writes

Drekkia Writes is a poet, an artist, the creator and energy curator, and CEO of Seven of Arts, an educational consulting firm. She is a published author of "17 Mirrors" and "The Art of Securing the Bag" and the founder of the women's empowerment organization Hey, Sis!

Writes is an award-winning spoken word artist. She formerly served as the Arts in Education Program Manager for the state of Arkansas. She currently serves as the youngest elected official on the Little Rock School District School Board and as a commissioner on the Arts + Culture Commission.

Her background is in teaching poetry and creative writing as a way to help modify behavior, to address social emotional learning, and to help increase literacy and communication skills. She is a graduate of the University of Central Arkansas where she studied Business Administration, Insurance and Risk Management.

She is also a radio personality on 96.5FM providing inspiration every Tuesday.

Writes' main focus in life is to entertain, educate, and empower the community through the arts.

Questions for Your Journey

Take what you need, throw away the rest!
-Amber Booth-McCoy

- Who did you want to be before they told you who to be?
- What does sisterhood mean to you?
- What does it look like in your life?
- Who pours into you? Do you return the love and energy?
- How will the women in your life remember you?
- What truth are you not telling yourself?
- What's a dream so big it scares you?
- For me to be me, I need….
- How can you be a better sister?
- Whose voice is the loudest in your head? If not yours, why?
- How will you work towards self-care?
- What does it mean to show up for yourself?
- When is the last time you felt powerful and why?
- When is the last time a song lyric stopped you in your tracks and resonated within your soul?
- What do you love about you? Why?